feed your
family for
£20 a week

in a hurry!

This book is dedicated to my beautiful
children Ayla, Jamie and Kyle. Nothing makes
me prouder than being your mum. I love you more
than life itself.

feed your
family for
£20 a week

in a hurry!

Lorna Cooper

SEVEN DIALS

Hi folks,

My name is Lorna Cooper and I run the Facebook community Feed Your Family for £20 a Week. I set it up six years ago, and it has since become an invaluable resource for anyone looking to eat well on a budget and wanting fuss-free food that's quick to make. I now have over half a million people visiting the page and following my tips and tricks, which is more than I could ever have hoped for when I started up from my living room in Paisley, Scotland.

My first cookbook, *Feed Your Family for £20 a Week*, came out in 2020 and the feedback was amazing. I have loved hearing how much you enjoy my delicious recipes, and how amazed you are that I manage to make such fab food from simple ingredients and on a tight budget.

As well as offering simple and tasty dishes, my mission is to provide tips and hacks that help household budgets go further. In times when we are all watching the pennies, you would be amazed at what you can buy for £20 a week and how far you can make those ingredients stretch. And it's not just about the meal you are planning for a particular day; buying the right ingredients in the correct quantities allows for my favourite money hack of all – repurposing leftovers! Rather than throwing away the remains of a family dinner, I will show you how to bulk out those leftovers with store cupboard essentials and turn them into lunch for the following day.

What I hope this book helps you to do is shop smartly and know exactly where your money is going. It's amazing how having a detailed list and meal plan as you browse the supermarket aisles can make all the difference.

Alongside savvy shopping, I will also give you tips on how best to store some foods to make them last the maximum amount of time and stop waste. From freezing fresh vegetables as soon as you get home from the supermarket, to never storing your potatoes and onions together without an apple to separate them – this book will help ensure every penny you spend counts for more.

So many of you have told me how one of the biggest challenges about cooking from scratch is the time constraint. I get it; as a mother of three and stepmother of two, I know exactly what it's like to have a hectic household with lots of mouths to feed, and often, after a long day, it's hard to find the motivation to start following a long and complicated recipe.

That's why, in *Feed Your Family for £20 A Week... In A Hurry!*, I have focused on wholesome, deliciously simple meals that can either be on the table in 20 minutes or require less than 20 minutes' prep with some hands-off cooking time. As with my previous book, I promise everything you need for seven days of family meals can be bought for £20 a week without exception, and I will show you how to shop cleverly, how to save money by cooking from scratch and how to make the most out of your leftovers by bulking out meals later in the week.

Never has saving time AND money been so easy! After all, less cooking time means more family time (and a much-needed cuppa and relax!).

xx Lorna xx

CONTENTS

RIGHT, LET'S GET STARTED!

In order to feed your family for £20 a week, you will need to shop smartly and shop around. Not everyone has the time to do this, but I do my shopping at a handful of supermarkets and budget stores depending on what they have on offer. I know that might sound like a lot of effort, but you get out what you put in!

That said, if you don't have the time to shop around, you can still save a lot of money by bulk cooking, batch freezing, reusing leftovers and storing fresh ingredients smartly. All of this will make sure that you don't waste a single thing you pay for at the till. Here are some of my favourite storage tips, to help you make the most of your £20 a week.

SMART STORAGE

POTATOES

These should be stored in a cool, dry, dark place – preferably in a paper sack or cloth bag. They should NEVER be stored near onions as this can cause them to sprout. Also, putting an apple in with the potatoes helps to keep them fresh.

GARLIC

This can be stored in the same way as potatoes, but the easiest way to keep garlic fresh is to throw the peeled cloves in a food processor with a little water and then freeze the puree in an ice cube tray. Once frozen, you can pop the cubes out and save them in a freezer bag.

ONIONS

These can be chopped and frozen, but will also keep for months if you put them into the leg of an old pair of sheer tights. Simply pop one in and then twist the tights before adding another. Challenge yourself and see how many you can fit in one leg! Tie with string and hang up somewhere cool, dry and dark.

SPRING ONIONS

These are best stored with the roots in a small amount of water in a glass. Stick the glass on the windowsill next to your homegrown herbs!

GINGER

Can be frozen as is, then just cut off what you need when you need it, popping the rest straight back into the freezer.

SHOPPING LIST: LORNA'S LIFESAVERS

■ Stock cubes add instant flavour – adding a stock cube and some frozen veg to rice or noodles makes it a meal in its own right.

■ Instead of buying packs of egg noodles from the world food aisle, which typically cost £1, buy own-brand instant noodles, which can be as cheap as 14p. Throw away the seasoning sachets and just cook in water.

■ Cornflour is a saviour for thickening all types of sauces.

■ Keep an eye out for garlic/ginger/chilli pastes or purees on offer. I always snap them up when they're at a great price because they last forever and save so much time and effort when it comes to chopping or creating pastes.

■ Buy frozen veg – not only is it generally cheaper, but also you waste less because it doesn't go off, meaning you can have more variety on a weekly/ monthly basis. It's also pre-prepped, so the only effort involved is opening the freezer drawer and grabbing a good handful! Alternatively, if you have fresh veg, it can be prepped and frozen in advance. Have a look through the meal plan, spot which ingredients you need and get organised!

■ Steer clear of convenience items – as you probably will have noticed, buying diced chicken is often more expensive than buying chicken breasts and dicing them yourself. ALWAYS check the price per kg of things you are buying. By being a little bit organised, you can prep ingredients yourself quickly and easily – relieving pressure on your shopping budget.

- I always pick up a sack of potatoes when they're on offer. Then, while I'm unpacking my shopping, I stick four on a tray and put them in the oven to save time and energy later in the week. Once they're cooked, wrap well and freeze. Note: if you're following the meal plan, there are four hash recipes over the course of the week, so this is the perfect way to save time and money.

- The same applies to meat: if there's a great bargain to be had, buy in bulk, and when you get home, separate out what you need and cook it there and then before freezing. Some of my recipes call for cooked chicken or cooked ham, for example. Both can be cooked in the slow cooker, oven or on the stove, and then divided up and frozen until needed.

- Freeze milk or cream in ice cube trays or bags to add to soups and sauces, or to use for tea/coffee.

MY TOP TIME-SAVING HACKS

I hope the previous tips will come in handy when you're next trawling the supermarket aisles, but this book isn't just about saving money – time is precious, too! Whoever thought 24 hours in a day was long enough, I'll never know, so here are some of my favourite time-saving lifesavers:

- When you buy meat that you are going to freeze, have a think about how you will be cooking it and which dishes you are going to use it for. If you are making a curry, then dice the chicken before freezing it to save time later on. Try to remember to defrost frozen meat the night before and keep it covered in the fridge. If, like me, you often forget, then set a reminder on your phone.

- If you intend on roasting fresh veg, including potatoes, then make sure you parboil them first for minimal oven time. And while you're doing that, heat the roasting tray and oil in the oven to make maximum use of your 20 minutes.

■ For a quick and easy mid-week dinner, your slow cooker is key. Invest some time of an evening to prep the ingredients for the next day's dinner and put them in the fridge. Tip into the slow cooker in the morning and come home to a ready-made meal in the evening. But don't rest on your laurels: use the time saved to prep the next evening's dinner, and so on. Or, if you can spare the time once a week or once a month, prep lots of meals and put them in the freezer, ready to be defrosted and popped in the slow cooker whenever you need them.

■ If you are cooking pasta and adding veg to the dish, cook the pasta and veg together in the one pan – less washing up at the other end!

■ Prepare pancake batter the night before and store in the fridge overnight – this works for Yorkshire puds, too.

■ Fresh veg and potatoes can be peeled and prepped the night before and stored in a pot with cold water and a lid. Just refresh the water in the morning and again before cooking in the evening.

■ Blitz the outside slices of a loaf or any bread going stale in the food processor and freeze for handy breadcrumbs.

Roasting time for vegetables to keep meal prep under 20 minutes	
Green Beans	10 mins
Asparagus	12–15 mins
Summer Squash	15–20 mins
Broccoli	20–25 mins
Butternut Squash	20–25 mins
Parsnips	20–25 mins
Red and White Onions	25–30 mins
Carrots	25–30 mins
Cauliflower	25–30 mins
Sweet Potatoes	30–35 mins
White Potatoes	35–40 mins
Brussels Sprouts	35–40 mins

HOW I SHOP

When it comes to food shopping, people tend to shop either in one place for everything or in multiple places for the best prices. Well, you know what I do: I shop around, always! But that doesn't mean I spend hours and hours every week scouring the shops for bargains. I split it up. So, instead of an hour in the same shop each week, I spend an hour each week in a different shop. One week I will go to the supermarket and buy four weeks' worth of items that are the cheapest there. The following week I will go to the freezer shop and buy a months' worth of the items that are cheapest there. The week after that I will go to the market and buy all my fresh veg in bulk. And the final week I will go to the bargain shops and buy the items they have on offer. Every two or three months I will go to the Asian supermarket and buy a huge sack of rice and spices.

It took me a while to have an idea of which shops in my area had the cheapest items, and it will probably take you some time as well, but once you've got the knack, it is much easier – and cheaper – to shop this way.

The following shopping list covers eight weeks' worth of meals, and I am assuming that, apart from the basics, your cupboards, freezer and fridge are empty, so we are starting from scratch. The reason we are shopping for eight weeks is that it gives us the opportunity to have the widest variety in the ingredients we use, and helps us take advantage of the cheapest prices by bulk buying.

Unfortunately, I'm writing this in lockdown, when it hasn't been the easiest time to find the best prices, although ingredient costs still vary wildly depending on where you live. Whether you want to commit the time and energy into shopping around to get similar prices to mine will depend on your personal circumstances. After the pandemic, we're heading into uncertain economic times and for some of you, sticking to the budget will be really important, meaning you'll put in the energy to shop around. For others, your time will be more precious and you won't mind paying a little extra for the convenience of buying from one place. Of course, there will be some of you who don't follow the plan at all and just want to dip in and out of the recipes. Every approach is fine, and no matter how you use this book, I hope you'll save time AND money. So grab your shopping bags and your purse, because we're heading to the shops!

SHOPPING LIST

FRESH VEG

3.5kg baby potatoes	£1.50
7.5kg potatoes	£2
8 bulbs of garlic	£1
5kg white onions	£2
700g mushrooms	£1
3.5kg cherry tomatoes	£3
6 lemons	£1.20
5 red chillies	£1
12 sweet potatoes	£1.50
3 courgettes	£1
1kg spring onions	£4
Ginger	50p
4 parsnips	42p
Celery	43p
7 carrots	39p
6 red onions	59p
9 bananas	£1.20
2 pears	45p
2 apples	40p
4 cucumbers	£1.40
6 tomatoes	50p
3 packs of mixed sweet peppers	60p
3 lettuces	£1.17

DAIRY

500g yoghurt	50p
2 x 300ml double cream	£1.70
150ml single cream	65p
150ml sour cream	75p
600ml crème fraîche	£1.79
6 x 200g soft cheese	£2.94
2 x 175g Grana Padano	£3.30
6 x 210g mozzarella cheese	£2.58
200g feta cheese	85p
750g butter	£2.97
4 x 550g mature Cheddar	£7.96
40 eggs	£1.96

FOOD CUPBOARD

2 x 1kg porridge oats	£1.50
1kg self-raising flour	45p
1kg plain flour	45p
5 x 500g dried pasta	£1.45
2 x 500g dried spaghetti	40p
6 x chicken noodles	84p
500g couscous	70p
4 x 1kg long grain white rice	£1.80
454g strawberry jam	28p
3 x 340g peanut butter	£2.55
Sun dried tomatoes	£1.09
Mandarins	59p
Pineapple chunks	65p
Peach slices	31p
2 x cannellini beans	£1.10
Baked beans	23p
Mixed beans	65p
Kidney beans	30p
2 x butter beans	72p
8 x chickpeas	£2.64
Corned beef	£1.45
2 x chopped tomatoes	56p
2 x tins of potatoes	£1
3 x tins of tuna chunks	£1.77
2 x tins of sardines	80p
Pink salmon	£1.80
3 x coconut milk	£2.07
1 litre orange juice	55p
18 x part-baked baguette 2-pack	£7.56
6 pitta breads	40p

MEAT & FISH

2 x 500g cooking bacon	£1.50
2 x 20 sausages	£2
2 x 400g cooked ham	£1.98
3 x smoked mackerel fillets	£4.47
200g chorizo	£1.49
1.5kg whole oxtail	75p

FROZEN MEAT & FISH

5 x 1kg chicken breasts	£15
3 x 900g bag of white fish fillets	£4.37
1.5kg thin-sliced beef	£3.50
3 x pork tenderloins	£5
500g chicken thigh fillets	£3

FROZEN VEG

950g sweetcorn	77p
900g broccoli florets	53p
900g cauliflower florets	53p

20 bags @ 5 for £4 = £16:

- 3 x 800g mixed peppers
- 3 x Mediterranean veg
- 2 x spinach
- 1 x baby carrots
- 1 x cabbage
- 2 x casserole veg mix
- 2 x butternut squash
- 2 x stir-fry veg
- 1 x leeks
- 2 x mixed veg
- 1 x peas

FROZEN FRUIT

9 bags @ 3 for £5 = £15:

- 1 x 500g pineapple chunks
- 1 x 500g blueberries
- 1 x 550g mango
- 1 x 650g strawberries
- 2 x 850g apples
- 2 x 650g raspberries

MISC

4 x 500g ready-made puff pastry	£2

– £7.50 off voucher

Total £160.18

STORE CUPBOARD

These items are all things I would expect to find in most people's store cupboards.
If they're not, they should be! Don't worry, we won't use them all up – just a teaspoon
here and there.

Ground coriander	Cayenne pepper	Cocoa powder
Chilli powder	Cajun seasoning	Cornflour
Ground cumin	Ground turmeric	Lime juice
Garlic powder	Garam masala	Lemon juice
Ground ginger	Cinnamon	Honey
Onion powder	Bay leaves	Mustard
Chilli flakes		Sweet chilli sauce
Paprika	Chipotle paste	Worcestershire sauce
Dried basil	Tomato puree	Light soy sauce
Dried Italian mixed herbs	Tomato ketchup	Hot sauce
Dried thyme	Mayonnaise	Apple cider vinegar
Curry powder	Salad cream	Balsamic vinegar
Curry paste	Stock cubes	White wine vinegar
Cumin seeds		Vegetable oil
Mustard powder	Pearl barley	
Mustard seeds	Split red lentils	Desiccated coconut
Onion salt		Vanilla essence
Celery salt	White sugar	Maple syrup
Dried oregano	Soft brown sugar	

GROWING YOUR OWN HERBS

I'll start this off by saying I am not much of a gardener, but I also hate
spending money on things that I don't need to spend money on. A few
years ago I bought myself lots of fresh herb pots from the supermarket
and replanted them into a long trough that now lives on my kitchen
windowsill. I make sure to water my herbs daily and pick the leaves in
the morning when they are at their best; always pick a mix of small and
larger leaves so as not to deplete the plant. There are plenty of guides
online on how to look after herb gardens, but the most common herbs are
actually really easy to look after. There is also something really satisfying
about producing something to eat yourself and, of course, it saves you
money! For the initial cost of a few pounds you can have fresh herbs
all year; or, even better, if you know someone who already grows their
own herbs, ask them for a few cuttings. Herbs used in this book: basil,
coriander, chives and parsley. I'd also recommend rosemary, thyme, mint
and oregano.

Week 1

Day	Breakfast	Lunch	Dinner
Sun	Sweet Potato Egg Nests (page 24)	Lorna's Signature Bruschetta (page 66)	Sausage Chilli (page 151)
Mon	Apple & Pear Muffins (page 26)	Smoked Mackerel Spread Sandwich (page 88)	Mexican Red Rice (page 109)
Tue	Blueberry Overnight Oats (page 30)	Tomato & Pesto Palmiers (page 84)	Broccoli Cheese Soup (page 58)
Wed	Apple & Pear Muffins (page 26)	Curried Egg Mayo Sandwich (page 88)	Beef Stroganoff (page 147)
Thu	Mint Choc Chip Smoothie (page 46)	Mexican Red Rice leftovers (page 109)	Tuscan Chicken Pasta (page 92)
Fri	Apple & Pear Muffins (page 26)	Broccoli Cheese Soup leftovers (page 58)	White Fish & Colcannon (page 154)
Sat	Pina Colada Overnight Oats (page 31)	Cheese & Onion Pasties (page 65)	Peanut Chicken (page 172)

Week 2

Day	Breakfast	Lunch	Dinner
Sun	Cheesy Ham Roll-ups (page 41)	Tuscan Chicken Pasta leftovers (page 92)	Honey Mustard Sausage Traybake (page 128)
Mon	Baked Oatmeal Cups (page 34)	Apple Slaw Sandwich (page 88)	Chicken Pilaf (page 114)
Tue	Chocolate & Banana Overnight Oats (page 30)	Tuna White Bean Salad (page 69)	Red Pepper & Tomato Soup (page 61)
Wed	Baked Oatmeal Cups (page 34)	Cheese Savoury Sandwich (page 89)	Philly Cheesesteak Baguettes (page 168)
Thu	Peach Cobbler Smoothie (page 46)	Chicken Pilaf leftovers (page 114)	Summer Pasta (page 98)
Fri	Baked Oatmeal Cups (page 34)	Red Pepper & Tomato Soup leftovers (page 61)	Salmon Hash (page 163)
Sat	Tropical Smoothie (page 44)	Tomato & Pesto Palmiers (page 84)	Beef & Potato Curry (page 183)

 When you see this icon in a recipe, freeze half of your batch in portions for a meal in the coming days or weeks. It appears in the meal plan as 'leftovers' when you'll eat those saved portions.

 When you see this, it means you'll be saving leftovers from the meal you have just cooked, to be used in a recipe later in the week or month.

 When you see this icon, it means you'll be using leftovers you saved while cooking a meal earlier in the plan.

Week 3

Day	Breakfast	Lunch	Dinner
Sun	Egg Clouds (page 20)	Summer Pasta Leftover Pasta Pizza (page 98/78)	Sweet Chilli Chicken Traybake (page 132)
Mon	Jam Crumble Bars (page 39)	Vegetarian Chickpea Sandwich (page 89)	Potato & Chickpea Rice (page 116)
Tue	Apple Pie Overnight Oats (page 31)	Salata (page 73)	Oxtail, Veg & Barley Broth (page 55)
Wed	Jam Crumble Bars (page 39)	Smoked Mackerel Spread Sandwich (page 88)	Lemon Chicken (page 144)
Thu	Green Smoothie (page 48)	Potato & Chickpea Rice leftovers (page 116)	One-pot Spicy Bacon & Tomato Pasta (page 101)
Fri	Jam Crumble Bars (page 39)	Oxtail, Veg & Barley Broth leftovers (page 55)	Summery Fish Stew (page 148)
Sat	Peanut Butter & Jelly Overnight Oats (page 31)	Soy & Honey Chicken Salad (page 70)	Veggie Sloppy Joes (page 192)

Week 4

Day	Breakfast	Lunch	Dinner
Sun	Sheet Pan Blueberry Pancakes (page 36)	One-pot Spicy Bacon & Tomato Pasta leftovers (page 101)	Maple-glazed Pork Traybake (page 136)
Mon	Cheese & Bacon Muffins (page 23)	Apple Slaw Sandwich (page 88)	Vegan Bean Burgers (page 191)
Tue	Blueberry Overnight Oats (page 30)	Sausage Roll Twists (page 82)	Ginger, Orange & Veg Soup (page 54)
Wed	Cheese & Bacon Muffins (page 23)	Cheese Savoury Sandwich (page 89)	Corned Beef Hash (page 158)
Thu	Raspberry Sunshine Smoothie (page 45)	Easy Pitta Bread Pizzas (page 80)	Chicken Pesto Pasta (page 106)
Fri	Cheese & Bacon Muffins (page 23)	Ginger, Orange & Veg Soup leftovers (page 54)	Tuna & Veg Risotto (page 122)
Sat	Apple Pie Smoothie (page 45)	Chicken Pesto Pasta Leftover Pasta Pizza (page 106/78)	Chipotle Chicken (page 176)

 When you see this icon, it means that meal is perfect to take out and about with you and eat on the go.

 I've included some add-ons throughout the book for if you're a bit flush with cash and feel like adding something extra special to your meal.

Week 5

Day	Breakfast	Lunch	Dinner
Sun	Cheesy Ham Roll-ups (page 41)	Tuna & Veg Risotto leftovers (page 122)	Beef & Chorizo Traybake (page 140)
Mon	Granola Bars (page 32)	Vegetarian Chickpea Sandwich (page 89)	Tangy Veggie Rice (page 110)
Tue	Peanut Butter & Jelly Overnight Oats (page 31)	Sausage Roll Twists leftovers (page 82)	Mushroom Soup (page 50)
Wed	Granola Bars (page 32)	Smoked Mackerel Spread Sandwich (page 88)	BBQ Pulled Chicken (page 167)
Thu	Berry Crush Smoothie (page 45)	Tangy Veggie Rice leftovers (page 110)	Stir-fried Pork Pasta (page 105)
Fri	Granola Bars (page 32)	Mushroom Soup leftovers (page 50)	Fish Curry (page 175)
Sat	Pina Colada Overnight Oats (page 31)	Stir-fried Pork Pasta leftovers (page 105)	Saucy Satay Chicken Noodles (page 186)

Week 6

Day	Breakfast	Lunch	Dinner
Sun	Sweet Potato Egg Nests (page 24)	Cheese & Onion Pasties leftovers (page 65)	BBQ Sausage Traybake (page 130)
Mon	Granola Bars (page 32)	Apple Slaw Sandwich (page 88)	Ham & Egg Rice (page 119)
Tue	Chocolate & Banana Overnight Oats (page 30)	Mediterranean Sardine Salad (page 74)	Butternut Squash & Chilli Soup (page 57)
Wed	Apple & Pear Muffins (page 26)	Curried Egg Mayo Sandwich (page 88)	Honey, Garlic & Soy Chicken Stir-fry (page 188)
Thu	Mint Choc Chip Smoothie (page 46)	Ham & Egg Rice leftovers (page 119)	Hidden Broccoli Pasta (page 95)
Fri	Apple & Pear Muffins (page 26)	Butternut Squash & Chilli Soup leftovers (page 57)	Steamed Fish with Couscous Parcels (page 157)
Sat	Berry Crush Smoothie (page 45)	Lorna's Signature Bruschetta (page 66)	Mandarin & Chickpea Curry (page 180)

Week 7

Day	Breakfast	Lunch	Dinner
Sun	Sheet Pan Blueberry Pancakes (page 36)	Hidden Broccoli Pasta Leftover Pasta Pizza (page 95/78)	Cajun Chicken Traybake (page 135)
Mon	Apple & Pear Muffins (page 26)	Smoked Mackerel Spread Sandwich (page 88)	Lemon Feta Rice (page 113)
Tue	Peanut Butter & Jelly Overnight Oats (page 51)	Tomato & Pesto Palmiers (page 84)	Crispy Pork Schnitzel (page 152)
Wed	Sheet Pan Blueberry Pancakes (page 36)	Cheese Savoury Sandwich (page 89)	Chorizo & Sausage Hash (page 164)
Thu	Peach Cobbler Smoothie (page 46)	Lemon Feta Rice leftovers (page 113)	Carbonara (page 96)
Fri	Sheet Pan Blueberry Pancakes (page 36)	Salata (page 73)	Cullen Skink (page 56)
Sat	Apple Pie Overnight Oats (page 31)	Carbonara Slices (page 77)	Sweet & Sour Veg Stir-fry (page 185)

Week 8

Day	Breakfast	Lunch	Dinner
Sun	Egg Clouds (page 20)	Cheese Savoury Sandwich (page 89)	Pork Loin Traybake (page 139)
Mon	Baked Oatmeal Cups (page 34)	Cullen Skink leftovers (page 56)	Golden Vegetable Rice (page 120)
Tue	Blueberry Overnight Oats (page 30)	Vegetarian Chickpea Sandwich (page 89)	Thick & Chunky Vegetable Soup (page 62)
Wed	Baked Oatmeal Cups (page 34)	Golden Vegetable Rice leftovers (page 120)	Ham Hash (page 160)
Thu	Tropical Smoothie (page 44)	Thick & Chunky Vegetable Soup leftovers (page 62)	One-pot Creamy Chicken Pasta (page 102)
Fri	Baked Oatmeal Cups (page 34)	Soy & Honey Chicken Salad (page 70)	Basil-crusted Fish Traybake (page 126)
Sat	Raspberry Sunshine Smoothie (page 45)	One-pot Creamy Chicken Pasta leftovers (page 102)	Lentil Dahl (page 178)

BREAKFAST
& SMOOTHIES

EGG CLOUDS

Basically, this is eggs on toast, but a couple of extra minutes in the prepping transforms this recipe into little fluffy clouds that will delight adults and children alike.

8 mins prep • 8 mins cooking time • Serves 4

4 eggs

Salt and pepper, to taste

Chilli flakes (optional)

Fresh chives, chopped (optional)

Preheat the oven to 180°C/Fan 160°C/Gas 4. Line a baking tray with baking paper.

Separate the egg whites from the yolks, leaving the yolks in their shells or in small bowls (one bowl per yolk is the best option). Make sure you don't break the yolks.

Add salt, pepper, some chilli flakes and chopped chives (if using) to the egg whites in a mixing bowl.

Whisk the whites until they are stiff.

Spoon the whites onto the baking tray, forming four 'clouds'.

With the back of your spoon, create a dent in the centre of each cloud and carefully place an egg yolk inside it.

Bake in the oven for 8 minutes or until the edges have turned golden brown.

TIP
Serve your eggy clouds on hot, buttery toast with a side of baked beans for a cooked breakfast with a difference.

CHEESE &
BACON MUFFINS

This yummy breakfast option is aimed at those with a savoury palette as opposed to a sweet tooth. The muffins provide a traditional breakfast taste with an interesting twist, and they also go great with soup.

5 mins prep • 15 mins cooking time • Makes 12

1 tsp oil

50g cooking bacon, diced

300g self-raising flour

¼ tsp cayenne pepper

100g grated cheese

2 tbsp fresh chives, finely chopped

3 eggs, lightly beaten

250ml milk

50g butter, melted

Preheat the oven to 200°C/Fan 180°C/Gas 6 and line a 12-hole muffin tin with paper cases.

Fry the bacon pieces in the oil until cooked and allow to cool.

Add the flour, cayenne pepper, cheese, chives and cooled bacon to a large bowl.

Make a well in the centre and add the wet ingredients – the eggs, milk and melted butter. Gently stir.

Divide the mixture evenly into the paper cases and bake in the oven for 15 minutes or until golden brown.

Leave to cool in the tin for 5 minutes before transferring to a wire rack to cool.

SWEET POTATO EGG NESTS

Although this is a simple and quick recipe, it gives the impression of being something a bit special. A perfect opportunity to wow any overnight guests.

....

2 mins prep • 13–18 mins cooking time • Makes 4

1 tbsp oil

¼ large sweet potato, peeled and finely grated

200g frozen baby spinach

4 eggs

Pinch of salt and pepper

Preheat the oven to 180°C/Fan 160°C/Gas 4 and grease four holes of a regular-sized muffin tin with the oil.

Using your fingers, line the greased muffin holes with the sweet potato, pressing to form a crust on the bottom and sides.

Bake the sweet potato crusts for 5–8 minutes, then remove from the oven.

Add the baby spinach on top of the sweet potato and crack an egg onto each crust.

Sprinkle with salt and pepper, and return to the oven to bake for a further 8–10 minutes, or until the egg whites are cooked.

TIP
A sprinkle of finely chopped, fresh chives will really top this one off – try growing your own (see page 13).

APPLE & PEAR MUFFINS

These light and tasty muffins make a great breakfast-on-the-go for parents and children alike. They can be prepped on a Sunday, stored in an airtight container and enjoyed all through the week.

10 mins prep • 20 mins cooking time • Makes 12

115g butter/margarine

115g caster sugar

2 eggs

115g self-raising flour

1 eating apple

1 pear

Preheat the oven to 180°C/Fan 160°C/Gas 4 and line a 12- hole muffin tin with paper cases.

Cream together the butter/margarine and sugar in a large bowl.

Beat the eggs, add to the bowl, then fold in your flour.

Peel, core and finely chop the apple and pear, then fold into the mixture.

Transfer the mixture to the muffin cases, divided evenly, and bake in the oven for 15–20 minutes.

The muffins are ready when they're golden brown and cooked through.

TIP

It's very important not to over-mix the mixture here, otherwise your muffins won't rise!

OVERNIGHT OATS

Often, despite our efforts to be healthier and eat a filling breakfast, many of us just don't have time in the morning to prepare such a thing. This is where overnight oats have revolutionised breakfast! But no one wants to eat the same thing every morning, so I have given you five different ways to enjoy this healthy start to the day.

5 mins prep • Serves 1

Place all the ingredients into a large glass container/bowl and mix until combined. Transfer to a jar or a glass. Cover and place in the fridge for at least 4 hours, or overnight. Top with extra fresh fruits/nuts/seeds and serve.

BLUEBERRY

45g porridge oats

45g fresh blueberries

Pinch of salt

70g plain yoghurt

1–2 tsp maple syrup

120ml milk

CHOCOLATE & BANANA

45g porridge oats

½ banana

1 tbsp cocoa powder

Pinch of salt

70g plain yoghurt

1–2 tsp maple syrup

120ml milk

Chocolate shavings and banana slices, for topping

> **TIP**
> Toasting seeds and nuts for the topping will add extra flavour – just pop them under the grill for a minute or two.

APPLE PIE

45g porridge oats

50g frozen apple, grated

Pinch of salt

70g plain yoghurt

1–2 tsp honey/maple syrup

120ml milk

½ tsp ground cinnamon

PINA COLADA

45g porridge oats

60g frozen pineapple chunks

1 tbsp desiccated coconut

Pinch of salt

70g plain yoghurt

1–2 tsp honey/maple syrup

120ml milk

½ tsp vanilla essence

Pineapple chunks and desiccated coconut, for topping

PEANUT BUTTER & JELLY

45g porridge oats

2 tbsp peanut butter

2 tbsp fruit jam

Pinch of salt

70g plain yoghurt

120ml milk

GRANOLA BARS

It's really easy to grab a granola bar in the morning, but they can be expensive so I decided to make my own. Three or four attempts later . . . success! Not only is it cheaper, but they are also healthier and tastier. Easy Sunday prep, then leave in the fridge to set and these are good to go.

....

15 mins prep • Makes 16

150g porridge oats

1 tsp ground cinnamon

½ tsp salt

200g add-ons (nuts, seeds, chocolate, shredded coconut or dried fruit)

250g peanut butter

300g honey

1 tsp vanilla essence

Line a 23cm square baking tin with two strips of criss-crossed baking paper, cut to fit neatly against the base and sides. This makes it easier to remove the bars later.

Place the oats in a large mixing bowl. Add the cinnamon and salt, and stir to combine. Set aside.

Blitz your chosen add-ons briefly in the food processor or blender: add any large nuts first and blitz for a few seconds, then add the rest and blitz until the ingredients are broken up into pieces smaller than your pinkie nail. Pour the add-ons into the bowl of oats.

In a jug, measure out the peanut butter. Top with the honey and vanilla essence. Stir until well blended. If the ingredients aren't blending easily, you can gently warm the liquid mixture on the stovetop or in the microwave, but make sure it's close to room temperature before you pour it into the dry mixture.

Pour the liquid ingredients into the dry ingredients. Mix until they are evenly combined and no dry oats remain. If the mixture is easy to mix, sprinkle in more oats until you can't incorporate any more. Transfer the mixture to the baking tin, arranging it fairly evenly, then use the bottom of a sturdy drinking glass to pack the mixture down as firmly and evenly as possible.

Cover the tin and refrigerate for at least one hour, preferably overnight. (The oats need time to soak up the moisture so they aren't sticky.) When ready, get it out of the tin by lifting both pieces of baking paper on opposite corners. Slice the bars into four columns and four rows.

Wrap individual bars in cling film or baking paper (if you store them together, they will stick to one another). The bars keep well for several days at room temperature, a couple of weeks in the fridge, or several months in the freezer.

BAKED OATMEAL CUPS

This fab grab-and-go breakfast is perfect for the whole family. The syrup and jam give an initial hit of energy, which is then followed up with long-lasting fuel from the oats. Prep on Sunday, and store in an airtight container to keep the cups fresh all week.

5 mins prep • 8 mins cooking time • Makes 12

250g porridge oats

250g peanut butter

170g maple syrup

1 tsp vanilla essence

65g plain flour

12 tsp jam

Preheat the oven to 180°C/Fan 160°C/Gas 4. Line a 12-hole muffin tin with baking paper, or grease.

Mix all your ingredients, except the jam, in a large bowl.

Place 1 tablespoon of the oat mixture at the bottom of each hole in the tin, then press it down with your hands. Leave some of the oat mix behind for the top of the cups.

Put 1 teaspoon of jam in the middle of each cup, then sprinkle the rest of the oat mix on top.

Bake in the oven for 8 minutes. Allow to cool in the tin before eating.

SHEET PAN BLUEBERRY PANCAKES

This pancake is as delicious as freshly made pancakes without the hassle of having to cook a new batch every morning – aren't I good to you? And you don't just have to stick with blueberries, any frozen fruit will do.

....

5 mins prep • 15 mins cooking time • Makes 15

380g plain flour

2 tbsp baking powder

2 tbsp sugar

2 tsp salt

600ml milk

2 eggs, beaten

6 tbsp butter, melted

200g frozen blueberries (or the fruit of your choice)

Preheat the oven to 220°C/Fan 200°C/Gas 7.

Line a half sheet pan (about 46 x 33cm) with greased baking paper.

In a large mixing bowl add the flour, baking powder, sugar and salt, and stir until well combined.

Add the milk, beaten eggs and melted butter, and stir until smooth and combined.

Pour the batter onto the prepared half sheet pan and spread it into an even layer with a rubber spatula.

Sprinkle the blueberries over the top.

Bake in the oven for 15 minutes. Allow to cool for a few minutes before slicing into 15 equal pieces (3 columns by 5 rows), then serve.

TIP
Dust with icing sugar for extra sweetness.

JAM CRUMBLE BARS

Perhaps more of a pudding-in-a-bar than a traditional cereal bar, these fruity crumble bars came together better than I imagined. The only problem is having just one . . .

15 mins prep • 45 mins cooking time • Makes 16

210g plain flour

½ tsp baking powder

½ tsp salt

95g sugar

120g cold butter, cut into cubes

1 egg, lightly beaten

160g fruit jam

Icing sugar, to dust

Preheat the oven to 180°C/Fan 160°C/Gas 4.

Grease a 23 x 13cm loaf tin and line it with baking paper. Set aside.

Sift the flour and baking powder into a bowl, then add the salt and caster sugar.

Cut in the butter with a food processor or by hand, until the mixture resembles fine breadcrumbs.

Stir in the beaten egg with a fork. The mixture should be dry and crumbly, but should form a dough when pressed together.

Remove 100g of the dough for the topping, and press the remainder of the dough into the prepared tin. Spoon the jam over the top, spreading it out evenly. Crumble the reserved dough evenly over the top.

Bake in the oven for 40–45 minutes, until golden brown and the edges have begun to pull away from the sides of the tin.

Leave to cool completely on a wire rack. To serve, dust with some icing sugar and cut into squares.

CHEESY HAM ROLL-UPS

I haven't met a kid yet who doesn't love a cheesy ham roll-up, and they're especially great for baby-led weaning and toddlers. I always find myself making a few extra just for me, too!

3 mins prep • 6 mins cooking time • Makes 16

6 eggs

4 tsp water

Pinch of salt and pepper

2 tbsp butter

100g Cheddar cheese, grated

4 slices of ham

Whisk together the eggs, water, and the salt and pepper.

Melt half of the butter in a 25cm non-stick frying pan over a medium heat, then pour in half of the egg mixture, swirling to coat the bottom of the pan.

Cook for 1–2 minutes or until the eggs begin to set. Flip the mixture over and top with half of the grated cheese. Cook for a further 1 minute or until the eggs are fully set, then transfer the omelette to a cutting board. Repeat with the remaining butter, egg mixture and cheese to make another omelette.

Arrange two ham slices along the centre of each omelette. Roll up each omelette tightly to enclose the filling. Slice each roll into eight pieces.

> **TIP**
> Substitute mozzarella for Cheddar cheese, and cooked turkey or chicken slices for the ham for some tasty alternatives.

SMOOTHIES

One of my children wasn't interested in eating in the morning; however, it was a long way to lunchtime for a growing boy. Breakfast smoothies saved the day and soon became the norm in our house. By using frozen fruit, I was able to provide lots of different flavours to keep him interested.

....

5 mins prep • Serves 1–2

Just place your tasty ingredients into your blender and blitz until smooth.

TROPICAL

150g frozen mango chunks

150g frozen strawberries

1 frozen banana, sliced

150g ice cubes

250ml milk

125ml water

60ml orange juice

60g plain yoghurt

1 tsp honey

BERRY CRUSH

300g frozen mixed berries, such as raspberries, blueberries, blackberries, defrosted slightly

150g frozen strawberries, sliced, defrosted slightly

300ml orange juice

200g plain yoghurt

1 tbsp sugar

2 tsp vanilla essence

APPLE PIE

300g frozen apples, defrosted slightly

250ml milk

60g plain yoghurt

1 tsp ground cinnamon

¼ tsp ground nutmeg

1 tbsp honey

RASPBERRY SUNSHINE

100g frozen mango chunks, defrosted slightly

125g frozen raspberries, defrosted slightly

250ml orange juice

120g plain yoghurt

1 tbsp honey

1 tsp vanilla essence

MINT CHOC CHIP

1 banana, peeled

150g ice cubes

60ml milk

120g plain yoghurt

5g fresh mint leaves

2 tbsp cocoa powder

2 tbsp chocolate chips

Fresh mint, to garnish

PEACH COBBLER

Half tin of peaches

375ml milk

3 ice cubes

45g porridge oats

1 tsp ground cinnamon

GREEN

1 small tin pineapple chunks

250ml milk

120g vanilla yoghurt

2 handfuls of frozen spinach

TIP

To cool down on a hot summer's day, add ice (or extra ice) before you blend.

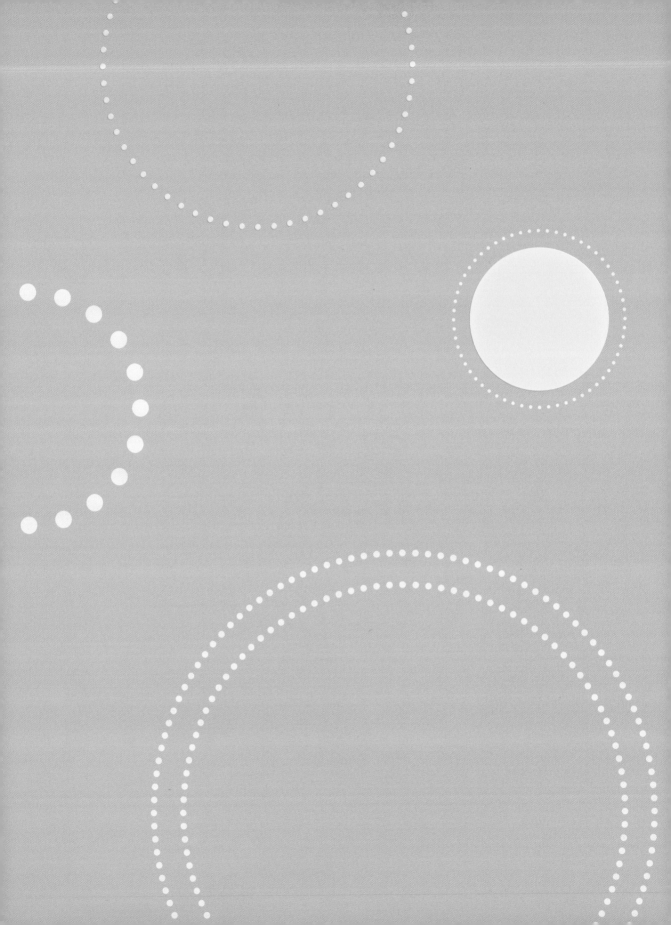

LUNCH
& SOUPS

MUSHROOM SOUP

There's something a little bit retro about mushroom soup. It's a classic dish that I'm happy to revisit regularly, and it can also be used as a base for casserole dishes or winter stews.

2 mins prep • 14 mins cooking • Serves 4 + 4 leftover portions

1 tbsp butter

1 onion, diced

1 celery stick, diced

1 potato, diced

2 garlic cloves, crushed

380g mushrooms, sliced

1.5l chicken stock

Salt and pepper, to taste

Crème fraîche, to serve

Part-baked baguette, to serve

Melt the butter in a large pot over a medium heat, then fry the onion, celery, potato and garlic for about 5 minutes.

Add the mushrooms and the stock, and bring to the boil.

Turn down the heat and simmer until the veg has softened, then remove from the heat.

Blitz with a hand blender to the desired texture, adding salt and pepper to taste.

Serve with a dollop of crème fraîche, and a part-baked baguette

> **TIP**
> Store any leftover soup in the freezer so that it's on standby for when you need a ready-made casserole sauce.

SLOW COOKER GINGER, ORANGE & VEG SOUP

I first encountered this dish in a posh restaurant with my sister – I was so intrigued
I just had to try it. Luckily, it was lovely, so I did my usual of trying to recreate it,
and here we have the finished article. I hope you like it, too.

10 mins prep • 4–8 hours cooking • Serves 4 + 4 leftover portions

1kg frozen casserole veg

4 parsnips, peeled and
chopped

1 tbsp grated ginger

300ml orange juice

1l vegetable stock

200ml double cream

Salt and pepper, to taste

Part-baked baguette, to
serve

Add all the ingredients, except the cream and seasoning,
to the slow cooker and mix well, then cover and cook on
high for 4 hours or on low for 8 hours.

Remove from the heat and whizz with a hand blender
until smooth.

Stir in the cream and season well with salt and pepper,
then serve with a part-baked baguette.

> **TIP**
> Remember to save half
> of this in the freezer for
> another day, just defrost
> in the fridge overnight
> before reheating
> and eating!

SLOW COOKER OXTAIL, VEG & BARLEY BROTH

Oxtail is comfort food for your soul. This is a rich, filling broth with a deep flavour – perfect for the winter months.

10 mins prep • 4–8 hours cooking • Serves 4 + 4 leftover portions

1.5kg oxtail, whole

500g frozen casserole veg

2 large potatoes, diced

1.5l beef stock

2 tbsp Worcestershire sauce

200g pearl barley

2 bay leaves

Salt and pepper, to taste

Part-baked baguette, to serve

Add everything to the slow cooker and mix well, then cover and cook on high for 4 hours, or on low for 8 hours.

Remove the oxtail, strip off and dice the meat and return it to the broth.

Remove the bay leaves, season to taste and then serve with a part-baked baguette.

TIP
Remember to save half of this in the freezer for another day, just defrost in the fridge overnight before reheating and eating!

SLOW COOKER CULLEN SKINK

This is one of Scotland's most famous dishes, coming from the small town of Cullen in north-east Scotland. If you're a seafood lover, then this is for you.

10 mins prep • 4–8 hours cooking • Serves 4 + 4 leftover portions

500g frozen leeks

2 onions, diced

4 potatoes, diced

400g white fish fillets, chopped

200ml milk

300ml water

50ml single cream

½ tsp salt

½ tsp pepper

Part-baked baguette, to serve

Add everything to the slow cooker and mix well. Then cover and cook for 4 hours on high, or for 8 hours on low.

Serve with a part-baked baguette.

TIP
Garnish with a little chopped fresh parsley – see page 13 for growing your own.

SLOW COOKER BUTTERNUT SQUASH & CHILLI SOUP

This soup is naturally thick and creamy, with a complementary kick from the chilli flakes. Ideal for autumn, when squash is available in abundance.

10 mins prep • 4–8 hours cooking • Serves 4 + 4 leftover portions

2 onions, diced

1 garlic clove, thinly sliced

2 tbsp chilli flakes

1kg frozen butternut squash

1.5l vegetable stock

4 tbsp crème fraîche

Part-baked baguette, to serve

Add all the ingredients, except the crème fraîche, to the slow cooker and mix well. Cover and cook on high for 4 hours or on low for 8 hours.

Remove from the heat and stir in the crème fraîche.

Blend with a hand blender until smooth, then serve with a part-baked baguette.

TIP
Sprinkle with extra chilli flakes for added impact.

BROCCOLI CHEESE SOUP

This is creamy comfort in a bowl, like a warm blanket of tasty cheesiness.

....

4 mins prep • 14 mins cooking • Serves 4 + 4 leftover portions

3 tbsp butter

2 onions, coarsely
chopped

6 garlic cloves, crushed

½ tsp chilli flakes (plus
optional extra to serve)

Salt and pepper, to taste

900g frozen broccoli

1 large potato, peeled and
cut into small chunks

1.5l water

250g mature Cheddar
cheese, grated

Fresh chives, chopped
(optional)

Part-baked baguette, to
serve

Melt the butter in a large soup pot over a medium-low heat. Add the onions, garlic, chilli flakes, salt and pepper.

Stir to combine, then cover the pot and cook, stirring occasionally, for about 5 minutes, until the onions have softened and are just starting to turn golden.

Add the broccoli and potato to the pot and stir. Pour in the water. Raise the heat to high and bring the mixture to the boil, then reduce the heat to medium-low and cover the pot. Cook for another 4–7 minutes, until the broccoli is bright green and easily pierced by a fork and the potato is soft.

Blend the soup with a hand blender until smooth.

Add almost all of the grated cheese (reserve a small handful) and stir until melted. Taste carefully – it's hot – and stir in more cheese if you'd like a more indulgent flavour/creamy texture and more salt and/or pepper for extra kick.

Divide the soup into bowls and top with a sprinkle of the remaining cheese, plus some chopped chives and/or more chilli flakes, if desired. Serve with a part-baked baguette.

SLOW COOKER RED PEPPER & TOMATO SOUP

How could you possibly go wrong with this soup? Tomatoes and red peppers
are a natural fit and create a rich soup to warm the cockles.

10 mins prep • 4–8 hours cooking • Serves 4 + 4 leftover portions

1 onion, finely diced

2 red peppers, chopped

1 tbsp oil

1.5l vegetable stock

2 tins chopped tomatoes

2 garlic cloves, crushed

Salt and pepper, to taste

A dash of cream (optional)

Part-baked baguette, to
serve

Add all the ingredients, except the cream, to the slow
cooker and mix well. Cover and cook on high for 4 hours
or on low for 8 hours.

Blitz with a hand blender, check the seasoning, add in a
little cream, if desired, and stir through.

Serve with a part-baked baguette

TIP
Remember to save half
of this in the freezer for
another day, just defrost
in the fridge overnight
before reheating
and eating!

SLOW COOKER THICK & CHUNKY VEGETABLE SOUP

Everybody should enjoy this hearty soup. My nana used to say 'a thick soup will stick to your ribs', which just means it's guaranteed to fill you up. She was right!

10 mins prep • 4 hours cooking • Serves 4 + 4 leftover portions

2 large potatoes, peeled and cut into chunks

4 carrots, chopped into large chunks

2 onions, cut into wedges

300g frozen mixed peppers

2 tins chopped tomatoes

2 garlic cloves, finely sliced

2l vegetable stock

100g pearl barley

Salt and pepper, to taste

Part-baked baguette, to serve

Add all the ingredients to the slow cooker, mix well then cover and cook for 4 hours on high.

When cooked, move most of the veg (except the potatoes) and pearl barley to a mixing bowl with a slotted spoon.

With a hand blender, whizz up the potatoes and remaining veg to thicken the soup.

Return the reserved veg and pearl barley to the soup.

Check the seasoning and add more to taste.

Serve with a part-baked baguette.

TIP
Remember to save half of this in the freezer for another day, just defrost in the fridge overnight before reheating and eating!

CHEESE & ONION PASTIES

When I was younger, I used to buy these from a well-known bakery chain, and I always loved them. Faced with some leftover mashed potato one day, I thought I'd have a go at making my own. Now I can have them any time I want, for much cheaper, and so can you.

....

5 mins prep • 15 mins cooking • Makes 6

3 potatoes, mashed

150g Cheddar cheese, grated

1 onion, finely diced

¼ tsp mustard

Plain flour, for dusting

500g ready-made puff pastry

1 egg, beaten

TIP
For a Cornish pasty, just replace the cheese with cooked beef.

Preheat the oven to 220°C/Fan 200°C/Gas 7. Grease a large baking tray.

In a large bowl, combine the mashed potato, cheese, onion and mustard.

Sprinkle a little flour on the work surface and roll out the pastry to the thickness of a 10-pence coin.

Cut out six circles from the pastry. I used a side plate (15cm diameter), but you can choose your own cutting tool to suit the desired size.

Place the pastry circles on the baking tray. Put a large spoonful of the mixture onto each circle, just slightly off-centre.

Fold each pastry circle over, sealing tightly around the edges using a fork.

Once you have sealed all of the pasties, brush the tops with the beaten egg.

Bake in the oven for 15 minutes, until golden and crispy.

LORNA'S SIGNATURE BRUSCHETTA

The simple yet flavoursome ingredients of this recipe come together beautifully.
It's so good, I put my name to it.

....

2 mins prep • 10 mins cooking • Serves 6

2 part-baked baguettes

200g cherry tomatoes,
 chopped and seeds
 removed

½ red onion, finely diced

2 garlic cloves, crushed

5 fresh basil leaves,
 chopped

1 tbsp oil, plus extra for
 brushing

¼ tsp salt

¼ tsp pepper

120ml balsamic vinegar

2 tbsp oil

½ tsp garlic powder

Bake the baguettes and allow to cool.

In a large bowl, combine the tomatoes, red onion, garlic, basil, oil, salt and pepper. Give it all a good mix with your hands.

If you have time, place the bowl in the fridge for 1 hour, to let the flavours come together.

In a small pot, heat the balsamic vinegar over a medium heat. Bring to the boil, reduce the heat and let it simmer for 5 minutes, until the liquid has reduced by half. Remove from the heat and leave to thicken.

In a small bowl, mix the oil with the garlic powder.

Cut the baguettes into slices just over 1cm in thickness.

Brush both sides of the slices with the oil/garlic mixture and lightly grill them.

Top each slice with some of the tomato mixture, then drizzle the balsamic glaze over them to serve.

TUNA WHITE BEAN SALAD

This salad is packed with healthy oils and protein, and is very simply but effectively flavoured with lemon and basil.

....

10 mins prep • Serves 4

2 tins cannellini beans

1 tin tuna in oil

1 red onion, finely chopped or thinly sliced

1 lemon

Salt and pepper, to taste

A large handful of fresh basil

2–3 tbsp olive oil

Drain and rinse the cannellini beans and place them in a large bowl. Drain the tuna and add to the bowl.

Add the red onion to the bowl. Grate the zest of the lemon over the mixture, then squeeze over the juice of half the lemon. Season with salt and pepper.

Finely chop the basil, keeping back a few leaves for garnish, and add to the bowl along with the olive oil (add more if desired). Stir everything until combined, garnish and enjoy!

TIP

Grow your own basil and save the pennies – see page 13.

SOY & HONEY CHICKEN SALAD

This light and tasty but filling dish is perfect for lunch, or even as a substantial starter.

2 mins prep • 8 mins cooking • Serves 4

120g salad leaves, washed and torn

350g cherry tomatoes, washed and halved

1 tbsp sesame oil

1 tbsp sunflower oil

250g cooked chicken, chopped

2 tbsp soy sauce

2 tbsp honey

Salt and pepper, to taste

Divide the salad leaves and tomatoes evenly between four plates.

Heat the two oils together in a large frying pan.

When the oils are really hot, place the chicken in the pan, add the soy sauce, lower the heat and stir to coat all the chicken pieces in the soy sauce.

After 5 minutes, add the honey and stir to coat all the chicken pieces.

Simmer the chicken for a couple of minutes.

Lift the pieces out one-by-one with tongs and share them out onto the four beds of salad.

Stir the leftover sauce in the pan and drizzle carefully over each salad.

Season to taste and serve immediately.

TIP

Swap out the chicken for cooked chicken livers or tinned mackerel for an equally tasty salad.

SALATA

This is a delicious, light, fresh and tangy salad. In the summer,
I'd be happy to eat this every day.

....

10 mins prep • Serves 4

3 tomatoes, diced

1 green pepper,
    deseeded and chopped

½ cucumber, deseeded
    and chopped

5 spring onions, white
    and green parts
    chopped

5g fresh parsley, chopped

1 small onion, chopped or
    thinly sliced

¼ lettuce, chopped/
    shredded

FOR THE DRESSING:

3 tbsp olive oil

3 tbsp lemon juice

2 garlic cloves, crushed

1 tsp dried mint

½ tsp salt

Black pepper, to taste

In a large bowl, mix the tomatoes, green pepper, cucumber, spring onions, parsley and onion.

In a mason jar or small bowl, combine the ingredients for the dressing. Seal the jar and shake the dressing, or whisk if using a bowl, until combined.

Pour the dressing over the salad and toss to combine. Taste, and adjust the mint, salt and pepper accordingly.

In the bowl with the salad, add the cos lettuce and toss to combine. Alternatively, you can lay a bed of lettuce in a serving bowl and add the salad on top.

feelin' fancy?

Goes great with cooked meat or tinned fish.

MEDITERRANEAN SARDINE SALAD

Who said salad has to be boring? It's all about getting the right mix of flavours to deliver a balanced yet tasty meal, and the addition of sardines here will transport you straight to the sunny Med.

10 mins prep • Serves 4

1 tin mixed beans

½ cucumber, chopped

150g cherry tomatoes, halved

1 red onion, diced

6 spring onions, chopped

50g sweetcorn

8 large lettuce leaves

2 tins sardines, drained

2 tbsp chopped fresh parsley

FOR THE DRESSING:

3 tbsp oil

1 tbsp white wine vinegar

2 tsp lemon juice

2 garlic cloves, crushed

½ tsp dried basil

¼ tsp chilli flakes

Pinch of dried oregano

Combine the (drained and rinsed) beans, cucumber, tomatoes, red onion, spring onion and sweetcorn in a mixing bowl.

Mix all the dressing ingredients together, then stir through the salad mixture.

Share out the salad mixture onto the top of each lettuce leaf.

Flake two or three sardine fillets on top of each salad, followed by some chopped parsley.

CARBONARA SLICES

Carbonara slices are a unique way of using up that leftover carbonara from page 96 – by binding the leftovers and oven-cooking them, they become a dish in their own right.

....

20 mins • Serves 4

3 eggs

200g soft cheese

20g Grana Padano (or any Italian hard cheese), grated, plus extra to serve

1 large courgette, grated

Leftover carbonara from page 96

250g cherry tomatoes

Grease and line an 11 x 26cm loaf tin with baking paper.

In a bowl, combine the eggs, soft cheese, 20g Grana Padano, courgette and leftover carbonara from page 96.

Spread into the prepared tin, then push in the cherry tomatoes and sprinkle over some more Grana Padano.

Bake in the oven for 15 minutes or until golden. Leave to cool, then cut into slices for a lunchbox treat.

LEFTOVER PASTA PIZZA

It's the two best things from Italy, so what could go wrong? Nothing, that's what!
I just don't know why anybody hasn't thought of this before.

5 mins prep • 14 mins cooking • Serves 4

500g leftover pasta, cold
  or room temperature

1 large egg

30g breadcrumbs

350g mozzarella cheese,
  grated

Salt and pepper, to taste

1½ tbsp oil

2 tbsp Grana Padano (or
  any Italian hard cheese),
  grated

If using spaghetti or long-shaped pasta, chop it up.
Put the pasta in a large bowl.

Add the egg, breadcrumbs, half of the mozzarella, and
salt and pepper. Mix well to combine.

Add the oil to a non-stick frying pan and swirl it around.
Add the pasta mixture and spread it out, while packing
it down tight to cover the base.

Place the pan over a high heat, then lower to a medium-
low heat as soon as you hear the oil sizzle. Let the pizza
continue to cook for about 2 minutes. Sprinkle the rest of
the mozzarella and the Grana Padano over the top.

Place the pan under a preheated medium grill until the
cheese is bubbling, then set the pizza, still in the pan,
aside to cool slightly.

After about 3–5 minutes, loosen the pizza edges with a
rubber spatula and gently transfer the pizza onto a cutting
board. Cut into slices and serve.

TIP
Scatter some
homegrown fresh
basil leaves (see
page 13) on top to
garnish your
pasta pizza.

EASY PITTA BREAD PIZZAS

Everybody loves pizza, right? But we don't always have time to make a pizza base. Using a pitta bread is an easy cheat for a quick and tasty lunch.

5 mins prep • 10 mins cook • Serves 4

4 pitta breads

2 tbsp tomato puree

200g mozzarella cheese, grated

Extra toppings of your choice (optional)

Preheat the oven to 180°C/Fan 160°C/Gas 4.

Prepare any toppings you want to add to your pizza. Leftover cooked meat/veg are great for these.

Place the pitta breads on an baking tray, then spread a thin layer of tomato puree over the top of each one, going right up to the edges.

Sprinkle over the mozzarella, again going right up to the edges.

Add your pizza toppings (if using). You can arrange them in fun shapes (faces are always a hit with the kids) or sprinkle them evenly – it's entirely up to you.

Bake in the oven for 8–10 minutes, until the cheese is melted and bubbling.

Leave to cool for a few minutes, then serve whole or cut into slices.

TIP
Scatter some fresh basil leaves on top (see page 13) and drizzle some olive oil over for a touch of authenticity.

SAUSAGE ROLL TWISTS WITH TOMATO DIP

These sausage rolls are my twist on an old favourite. Not as heavy as a traditional sausage roll, when served with the dip these are great for parties and picnics.

10 mins prep • 25 mins cook • Makes 8

500g ready-made puff pastry

Plain flour, for dusting

8 sausages

Beaten egg or milk, for brushing

FOR THE TOMATO DIP:

6 tbsp tomato ketchup

2 tsp vinegar

6 cherry tomatoes, finely chopped

Preheat the oven to 200°C/Fan 180°C/Gas 6.

On a lightly floured surface, roll out the pastry to a £1-coin thickness and into a 20 x 30cm rectangle. Cut into eight strips, each about 1cm wide, cutting from the shorter edge. Let the pastry come up to room temperature, otherwise it will shrink and split during baking.

Wind one pastry strip around each sausage, then place on a baking tray, pastry ends down. Brush with beaten egg or milk.

Bake in the oven for 25 minutes, keeping an eye on progress, until the sausages are cooked and pastry is golden.

Meanwhile, for the dip, mix together the ketchup, vinegar and cherry tomatoes. Serve in a little bowl alongside the twists.

TOMATO & PESTO PALMIERS

Another great recipe for picnics, parties and lunchboxes, these French pastries are simplicity at its best. It's amazing what you can do with so few ingredients.

5 mins prep • 15 mins cook • Makes 12

250g ready-made puff pastry

Plain flour, for dusting

100g pesto

100g sundried tomatoes, drained and finely chopped

Preheat the oven to 200°C/Fan 180°C/Gas 6. Line two baking trays with baking paper.

Roll the puff pastry out on a lightly floured surface, into a 25 x 30cm rectangle.

Spread the pesto evenly over the left-hand side of the pastry, then sprinkle the sundried tomatoes over the right-hand side of the pastry.

Roll the left-hand side of the puff pastry so that it meets the centre of the rectangle. Do the same with the right-hand side so that it meets the rolled left-hand side in the middle.

Cut slices across the rolled pastry, roughly 1cm thick.

Pinch the sides of the pastry slices so that they each form a classic palmier shape.

Transfer the palmiers to the baking trays, spaced well apart, and bake in the oven for 12–15 minutes, until golden.

Allow to cool slightly on a wire rack before serving.

SANDWICH FILLERS

Wave goodbye to boring old soggy sandwiches and say 'hellooo!' to these exciting, new fillings that will spice up your lunchbox. Just mix the ingredients by hand and you're ready to go.

....

5 mins prep • Serves 4

APPLE SLAW

4 tbsp mayonnaise

1 tbsp lemon juice

50g Cheddar cheese, grated

50g frozen apple, grated or chopped

4 spring onions, sliced

Black pepper, to taste

CURRIED EGG MAYO

4 hard-boiled eggs, cooled, peeled and chopped

1 tsp curry paste

1 tbsp mayonnaise

1 tsp tomato puree

4 spring onions, diced

6 slices of cucumber, diced

> **TIP**
> Sprinkle some homegrown chopped fresh parsley (see page 13) into the mix.

SMOKED MACKEREL SPREAD

180g smoked mackerel, flaked

200g soft cheese

1 tsp lemon juice

3 tsp chives

Salt and pepper, to taste

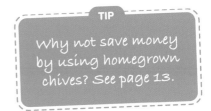

TIP

Why not save money by using homegrown chives? See page 13.

VEGETARIAN CHICKPEA

1 tin chickpeas, drained and rinsed

1 celery stick, chopped

½ onion, chopped

1 tbsp mayonnaise

1 tbsp lemon juice

Salt and pepper, to taste

CHEESE SAVOURY

250g Cheddar cheese, grated

1 large carrot, peeled and grated

1 large red onion, peeled and grated

Salad cream, to taste

Salt and pepper, to taste

PASTA & RICE

TUSCAN CHICKEN PASTA

This is an absolute banger. In fact, in my house we call it 'Bangin' Pasta'.
It tastes indulgent, creamy and perfect.

5 mins prep • 15 mins cooking • Serves 4 + 4 leftover portions

2 chicken stock cubes

400g pasta

2 tbsp dried Italian mixed herbs

1 tbsp oil

3 chicken breasts, diced small

Salt and pepper, to taste

4 tbsp garlic, crushed

350g cherry tomatoes, halved

200g cream cheese

50ml double cream

2 tins chopped tomatoes or 800ml tomato base sauce (page 217)

200g frozen baby carrots

200g frozen spinach

100g Grana Padano (or any Italian hard cheese), grated

Put a pot of water on for the pasta and once it begins to boil, add the chicken stock cubes. Stir until they have dissolved, then add the pasta and herbs, and cook as instructed on the pasta pack.

Meanwile, heat the oil in another large pot and add the chicken pieces. Season the chicken with salt and pepper, then brown all over.

Remove the chicken from the pot and set aside. Add the garlic and cherry tomatoes to the pot and cook for 1 minute.

Add the cream cheese, cream, tomatoes and carrots, and stir through.

Add the chicken back to the pot, reduce the heat and cook for 10 minutes.

Drain the pasta, reserving 250ml of the cooking water in a jug, and add to the pot along with the reserved cooking water (this helps the sauce stick to the pasta), spinach and Grana Padano.

Stir through and allow to cook for a few minutes, until the sauce has thickened and the spinach has warmed through. Serve.

TIP

Remember to save half of this in the freezer for another day, just defrost in the fridge overnight before reheating and eating!

HIDDEN BROCCOLI PASTA

Two of my three kids refused to eat broccoli . . . or so they thought. With the healthy green veg cooked and blitzed in this pasta, they were none the wiser.

3 mins prep • 17 mins cooking • Serves 4 + 4 leftover portions

400g frozen broccoli

400g pasta

350g frozen Mediterranean chargrilled veg

45g Parmigiano, grated

20g fresh basil leaves

3 tbsp oil

2 tsp lemon juice

Salt and pepper, to taste

Finely chop the broccoli florets, then cook in a pot of boiling water for about 3 minutes, until crisp–tender.

Using a slotted spoon, transfer the broccoli to a large bowl of iced water, then drain on paper towels.

Add the pasta to the same pot of boiling water and cook according to the packet instructions, until al dente. While the pasta cooks, stir-fry the chargrilled veg for 5 minutes, then set aside and transfer the broccoli (reserving a handful of florets) to a food processor.

Add the Parmigiano, basil, oil and lemon juice to the food processor. Season with salt and pepper, then blitz until smooth.

Drain the pasta, reserving 125ml of the pasta cooking water in a jug, and return the pasta to the pot. Toss the pasta together with the veg and broccoli pesto, adding the reserved pasta cooking water as needed to coat evenly.

Toss in the reserved broccoli florets (for those who will willingly eat them!), and season with salt and pepper.

TIP
Remember to save half of this in the freezer for another day, just defrost in the fridge overnight before reheating and eating!

CARBONARA

Carbonara is a classic quick dish, without sacrificing any of that all-important flavour. I've doubled the quantities here so you can use the leftovers to make the carbonara slices on page 77.

5 mins prep • 15 mins cooking • Serves 4 + 4 leftover portions

400g spaghetti

2 tbsp oil

250g cooking bacon, chopped

100g sliced mushrooms

3 garlic cloves, crushed

3 eggs

60g Grana Padano (or any Italian hard cheese), grated, plus extra to serve

Salt and pepper, to taste

½ bunch parsley, chopped

Cook the pasta according to the packet instructions.

Meanwhile, heat the oil in a frying pan over a medium heat. Cook the bacon and mushrooms, stirring, for 3–4 minutes, until the bacon begins to crisp. Add the garlic and cook for a further 30 seconds. Set the pan aside.

Place the eggs and Grana Padano (or other hard cheese) in a bowl. Season, and mix gently with a fork.

Drain the pasta, reserving 100ml of the water in a jug, then return the pasta to the pan. Quickly add the egg mixture, bacon and mushrooms, reserved water and parsley. Toss to combine – the heat from the pasta will cook the egg slightly and form a creamy sauce.

Set aside a quarter of the mixture in a bowl. Serve the remaining pasta for dinner, with extra Grana Padano.

TIP

Make carbonara slices from the leftovers – see page 77.

SUMMER PASTA

This dish makes me feel like I should be eating it on the patio
on a hot summer's day – hence the name.

4 mins prep • 14 mins cooking • Serves 4 + 4 leftover portions

400g pasta

250g frozen broccoli

2 medium courgettes
(about 200–250g)

25g butter

1 garlic clove, crushed

3 tbsp double cream

1 tbsp lemon juice, plus
extra to taste

Fresh parsley, chopped

Salt and pepper, to taste

100g Grana Padano (or
any Italian hard cheese),
grated

Cook the pasta as per the packet instructions but, towards
the end of the cooking time, add the broccoli as well.

Meanwhile, cut the top and bottom off the courgettes and
grate them coarsely.

Heat a large frying pan or wok, add the butter and let it
melt, then stir-fry the courgettes and garlic for 2 minutes,
until just cooked through.

Drain the pasta and broccoli, saving a little of the cooking
water in a jug, and return to the pan.

Pour over the cream and lemon juice, tip in the courgette/
garlic mixture and handful of chopped parsley, and mix
them through the pasta using a fork.

Stir in a spoonful or two of the reserved pasta cooking
water.

Check the seasoning, adding salt and pepper and extra
lemon juice to taste, then stir through the grated cheese
and serve.

TIP
Remember to save half
of this in the freezer for
another day, just defrost in
the fridge overnight before
reheating and eating!

ONE-POT SPICY BACON & TOMATO PASTA

What I love about pasta is the variety of flavours that can be served up from such a simple base. If your family is used to the taste of jars of sauce, you may want to add a teaspoon or two of sugar to this dish.

....

3 mins prep • 15 mins cooking • Serves 4 + 4 leftover portions

250g cooking bacon

1 tbsp oil

2 tbsp chilli powder

400g penne pasta

200g frozen mixed veg

2 tins chopped tomatoes
or 800ml tomato base
sauce (page 217)

250ml vegetable stock

200g frozen spinach

Chop the bacon into lardons. Add the oil to a large pot over a medium heat, then add the bacon and cook for 3–4 minutes.

Add the chilli powder and cook for 1 minute more.

Add the uncooked pasta, mixed veg, tomatoes and veg stock to the pot.

Put a lid on the pot, turn up the heat to medium-high and bring the stock to the boil.

Once the stock comes to a full boil, give the pasta a quick stir, add the spinach, replace the lid and turn the heat down to medium-low.

Let the pasta simmer for about 8 minutes, or until it is tender and most of the stock has been absorbed. Serve.

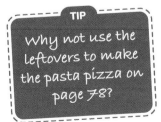

TIP

Why not use the leftovers to make the pasta pizza on page 78?

feelin' fancy?

Stir in some cream or cream cheese once the pasta is cooked.

ONE-POT CREAMY CHICKEN PASTA

As a busy mum, I love one-pot dishes – and the whole family devours this one, which is also delicious when served cold for lunch. Remember to save half of this in the freezer for another day, just defrost in the fridge overnight before eating or reheating it!

2 mins prep • 18 mins cooking • Serves 4 + 4 leftover portions

3 chicken breasts

2 tbsp butter

200g frozen leeks

2 garlic cloves, crushed

400g penne pasta

750ml chicken stock

200g frozen spinach

500ml milk

150g cream cheese

100g Grana Padano (or any Italian hard cheese), grated

Black pepper, to taste

Pinch of chilli flakes

Cut the chicken breasts into 2.5cm pieces. Add the butter to a large pot and melt over a medium heat. Add the chicken and leeks to the pan, and cook over a medium heat until the chicken is slightly browned on the outside.

Add the garlic to the pot with the chicken and continue to fry for 1 minute more.

Add the uncooked pasta and chicken stock. Stir to dissolve any browned bits from the bottom of the pot. Place a lid on the pot, turn the heat up to medium-high and bring the stock to the boil.

Once the stock comes to a full boil, give the pasta a quick stir, add the spinach, replace the lid and turn the heat down to medium-low.

Let the pasta simmer for about 8 minutes, or until the pasta is tender and most of the stock has been absorbed. Stir the pasta briefly every 2 minutes as it simmers, replacing the lid quickly each time.

Once the pasta is tender and most of the stock has been absorbed, add the milk and cream cheese (cut into chunks). Stir and cook over a medium heat until the cream cheese has fully melted into the sauce.

Add the grated Grana Padano and stir until combined. Top the pasta with black pepper and chilli flakes, then serve.

TIP

Just go with black pepper if your kids would object to the spiciness of chilli flakes.

STIR-FRIED PORK WITH CHILLI & GARLIC

Another pork dish with no apple or cider, this is not your run-of-the-mill dish.
Stir-fried pork in spaghetti may not sound like natural companions, but it works a treat.
Try it and see for yourself.

5 mins prep • 12 mins cooking • Serves 4 + 4 leftover portions

400g spaghetti

1 tbsp oil

½ tsp chilli powder, or to taste

2 garlic cloves, crushed

200g frozen cabbage

200g frozen leeks

200g frozen mixed peppers

100g frozen baby carrots

350g pork tenderloin, cubed

Cook the spaghetti according to the pack instructions.

Meanwhile, heat the oil in a large frying pan or wok over a medium heat and add the chilli powder, garlic and cabbage. Stir-fry for 2–3 minutes.

Add the rest of the vegetables to the cabbage and stir-gry for a further 2 minutes.

Add the pork, increase the heat and stir-fry for about 5 minutes, or until the pork is well cooked and the dish is piping hot.

Mix through the drained, cooked spaghetti then serve.

TIP

Remember to save half of this in the freezer for another day. Just defrost in the fridge overnight before reheating and eating!

CHICKEN PESTO PASTA

I often find pesto overpowering, but the crème fraîche here tones it down. The flavours complement one another perfectly. Remember to save half of this in the freezer for another day, just defrost in the fridge overnight before reheating and eating it!

2 mins prep • 12 mins cooking • Serves 4 + 4 leftover portions

400g pasta

Pinch of salt

200g frozen peas

200g frozen baby carrots

200g leftover cooked chicken, chopped

200ml crème fraîche

4 tbsp basil pesto (page 215)

50g Grana Padano (or any Italian hard cheese), shavings

Black pepper, to taste

Fresh basil leaves, to garnish

Cook the pasta in a large pan of salted, boiling water according to the packet instructions.

During the last 3 minutes of cooking time, add the frozen peas and carrots.

Drain well and return to the pan along with a little of the pasta water.

Stir in the cooked chicken, crème fraîche and pesto.

Cook for 1–2 minutes, until piping hot.

Serve topped with Grana Padano shavings and black pepper and garnish with basil leaves.

TIP

Save on pounds by growing your own basil – see page 13.

MEXICAN RED RICE

This is my partner John's favourite. It's a simple dish for a man with simple tastes.

5 mins prep • 20 mins cooking • 10 mins resting • Serves 4 + 4 leftover portions

1 tbsp oil

4 garlic cloves, crushed

1 tsp ground coriander

1 tbsp chilli powder

1 onion, finely chopped

450g long-grain white rice

1l chicken or vegetable stock

¼ tsp salt

2½ tbsp tomato puree

500g mixed veg

Heat the oil in a large saucepan over a medium heat. Add the garlic, coriander and chilli powder, stir briefly, then add the onion. Cook for 4 minutes.

Add the rice, stock, salt and tomato puree. Stir until the tomato puree has dissolved, then add the mixed veg.

Cover and bring to a simmer, then reduce the heat to low so the stock is simmering gently.

Cook for 15 minutes or until the liquid is absorbed (tilt the pot carefully to check).

Remove from the heat, leave the lid on and rest for 10 minutes. This is very important as the residual liquid on the surface of the rice will be absorbed and the rice will go from sticky to fluffy.

Fluff with a fork and serve.

TIP
Remember to save half of this in the freezer for another day, just defrost in the fridge overnight before reheating and eating!

TANGY VEGGIE RICE

This one will set your taste buds alight – it's a little punch of flavour
in a deceptively simple package.

2 mins prep • 16 mins cooking • Serves 4 + 4 leftover portions

3 tbsp oil

250g frozen casserole veg

400g long-grain white
rice

1l vegetable stock

1 tbsp curry powder

1 tbsp chilli powder

1 tsp ground turmeric

Pinch of salt and pepper

3 tbsp lime juice

100g frozen peas,
defrosted

Heat the oil in a saucepan over a medium heat, then add
the frozen veg and rice, and stir to coat.

Add the stock, curry powder, chilli powder, turmeric and a
pinch of salt and pepper to the saucepan, and cover.

Bring to the boil over a medium heat, then reduce the
heat to low and cook for 12 minutes or until the stock has
all been absorbed and the rice is tender.

Fluff the rice with a fork, add the lime juice and stir in the
defrosted peas, then serve.

TIP

Remember to save half
of this in the freezer for
another day. Just defrost in
the fridge overnight before
reheating and eating!

LEMON FETA RICE

On a Greek-island holiday a couple of years ago, I had a lemon feta rice dish. It took a few attempts for me to replicate it when I was back home, but now that I have, I want to share it with you. It's beautiful served hot or cold.

5 mins prep • 15 mins cooking • Serves 4 + 4 leftover portions

4 tbsp oil

2 onions, finely chopped

3 tsp dried oregano

3 large garlic cloves, finely chopped

1 tsp black pepper

450g long-grain white rice

1l chicken stock

1 tbsp lemon juice

200g crumbled feta cheese

Salt and pepper, to taste

Heat the oil in a saucepan over a medium-high heat.

Add the onions, oregano, chopped garlic and black pepper, then cook, stirring constantly, for about 2 minutes.

Add the rice and stir using a wooden spoon for 3 minutes.

Slowly pour in the stock and lemon juice, then bring to the boil.

Reduce the heat, cover, and simmer until the rice is tender (about 15 minutes).

Remove from the heat and stir in the feta cheese.

Season with salt and more black pepper, if desired.

> **TIP**
> Sprinkle some homegrown chopped fresh parsley (see page 13) into the mix.

feelin' fancy? Serve with a couple of lemon wedges to squeeze on top.

CHICKEN PILAF

Nothing beats a fail-safe pilaf recipe for a quick but nutritious midweek dinner.

3 mins prep • 17 mins cooking • Serves 4 + 4 leftover portions

1 tbsp oil

2 onions, chopped

150g frozen sliced carrots

3 garlic cloves, crushed

2 red chillies, finely
chopped (optional)

150g frozen peas

400g long-grain white
rice

250g leftover cooked
chicken, shredded

1l chicken stock

150g frozen spinach

Heat the oil in a large pan, then add the onions and carrots, and fry until they start to soften.

Add the garlic, chillies (if using), peas and rice, and stir to coat in the oil.

Stir in the chicken, then pour in the stock and gently bring to the boil.

Put a lid on the pan and simmer for 15 minutes.

Stir the spinach through and, once heated through, serve.

TIP

Remember to save half of this in the freezer for another day, just defrost in the fridge overnight before reheating and eating!

feelin' fancy?

If using chillies, keep some back to use as a garnish.

POTATO & CHICKPEA RICE

This is a real store cupboard special. I experimented by using up bits and pieces of this and that, which all came together perfectly in the end.

3 mins prep • 17 mins cooking • Serves 4 + 4 leftover portions

2 tbsp oil

1 tsp cumin seeds

2 garlic cloves, crushed

1 onion, thinly sliced

¼ tsp red chilli powder

½ tsp ground coriander

½ tsp ground cumin

Pinch of salt

2 tins chopped tomatoes or 800ml tomato base sauce (page 217)

1 tin chickpeas

400g long-grain white rice

100g frozen peas

100g frozen sweetcorn

100g frozen baby carrots

1l vegetable stock

2 tins potatoes

Heat the oil in a large pot and fry the cumin seeds, garlic and onion for 2 minutes.

Add the spices and salt, and fry for a few seconds.

Add the tomatoes and stir-fry for 1 minute before adding the (drained and rinsed) chickpeas. Mix well to coat the chickpeas with the spiced tomato mixture.

Add the rice, veg and stock, and stir to mix everything well.

Cover and bring to a rolling simmer, then cook until all the water is absorbed and the rice is cooked.

Fluff the rice with a fork, then add the (drained) potatoes and stir through. Serve.

> **TIP**
> Garnish with a handful of fresh coriander leaves, chopped – see page 13 for growing your own.

HAM & EGG RICE

This recipe is packed full of flavour and goodness. What more could you want?

2 mins prep • 18 mins cooking • Serves 4 + 4 leftover portions

1l ham stock

1½ tbsp soy sauce

1½ tbsp oil

¾ tsp ground ginger

1¼ tsp garlic powder

1¼ tsp onion powder

1 tsp salt

¼ tsp black pepper

400g long-grain white rice

150g frozen sweetcorn

150g frozen peas

4 eggs

200g cooked ham, diced

6 spring onions, chopped

Add everything except the eggs, ham and spring onions to a large pot, cover and bring to the boil, then reduce the heat.

Simmer the ingredients until the rice is cooked and the stock is all absorbed.

Meanwhile, hard-boil the four eggs in a separate pan (about 12 minutes), then set aside.

Stir the ham and spring onions into the large pot.

Peel and roughly chop the boiled eggs and serve on top of the ham rice.

> **TIP**
> Remember to save half of this in the freezer for another day. Just defrost in the fridge overnight before reheating and eating!

GOLDEN VEGETABLE RICE

You know those packets of flavoured rice in the supermarkets? Well, now you don't have to buy them. Save yourself a fortune and make the switch to homemade today.

2 mins prep • 18 mins cooking • Serves 4 + 4 leftover portions

1 tbsp oil

2 onions, diced

4 garlic cloves, finely chopped

1 tbsp chilli flakes (optional), plus extra to serve

150g frozen peas

150g frozen sweetcorn

400g long-grain white rice

1l vegetable stock

100g cherry tomatoes

Salt and pepper, to taste

Heat the oil in a large pan over a medium heat, add the onions and fry until softened and just starting to colour.

Add the garlic and chill flakes (if using), and fry for 1 minute more.

Tip in the frozen veg and rice, and stir until the rice starts to make slight popping sounds.

Pour in the stock and add the cherry tomatoes. Stir well and cover with a lid.

Bring to the boil, then reduce the heat and simmer for about 15 minutes, or until the rice is tender and the liquid has mostly been absorbed. Stir every so often so the rice doesn't stick to the bottom of the pan.

Season with salt and pepper to taste, and sprinkle with some more chilli flakes, if using.

TIP

Remember to save half of this in the freezer for another day, just defrost in the fridge overnight before reheating and eating!

TUNA & VEG RISOTTO

If you are a fan of risotto, you're gonna love this; if you're not a fan of risotto, you might be convinced otherwise! By using tinned tuna and frozen veg, the cost is low, but you wouldn't know it from the taste.

2 mins prep • 18 mins cooking • Serves 4 + 4 leftover portions

400g long-grain white rice

3 tbsp butter

200g frozen sliced leeks

2 garlic cloves, chopped

2 tbsp plain flour

375ml milk

100g cherry tomatoes, halved

4 spring onions, chopped

2 tins tuna, drained and flaked

100g frozen spinach

3 tbsp fresh parsley, chopped, plus extra for garnish

2 tbsp lemon juice

Salt and pepper, to taste

Rinse the rice and cook as per the packet instructions.

Meanwhile, melt the butter in a large saucepan over a medium heat. Fry the leeks in the butter for about 3 minutes, until they begin to soften. Then add the garlic and fry for 1 minute.

Add the flour to the saucepan and stir to incorporate it into the butter. If there is not enough butter in the pan to moisten the flour, add ½ tablespoon more. Cook the flour (roux) for about 5 minutes, stirring constantly.

Gradually pour the milk into the saucepan and whisk until a smooth sauce forms.

Bring gently to the boil and then simmer for 7 minutes, stirring constantly to prevent lumps forming in the sauce.

Add the tomatoes, spring onion, tuna, spinach and chopped parsley. Stir, and then simmer for 2 minutes.

Turn off the heat and stir in the lemon juice. Season with salt and pepper to taste.

Stir the tuna and veg sauce into the still-hot rice using a fork until well combined. Garnish with the extra parsley and serve.

TIP

Remember to save half of this in the freezer for another day, just defrost in the fridge overnight before reheating and eating!

TRAYBAKES

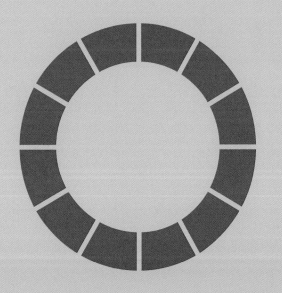

BASIL-CRUSTED FISH TRAYBAKE

Basil and fish make an excellent combo in this beautiful Mediterranean-inspired traybake, guaranteed to bring the sunshine to your table.

10 mins prep • 20 mins cooking • Serves 4

3 frozen white fish fillets, defrosted

100g breadcrumbs

Salt and pepper

2 tbsp dried basil

2 tbsp tomato puree

350g frozen Mediterranean veg

Oil, as needed

1 lemon, cut into 4 wedges

Part-baked baguette, to serve

Preheat the oven to 180°C/Fan 160°C/Gas 4.

Pat the fish dry with a paper towel and split one fillet in half (for the kids).

Mix the breadcrumbs with the seasoning and basil.

Spread a little tomato puree on top of each fillet. Top with the breadcrumb mix and pat it on.

Grease a baking tray, put the fillets and veg on the tray, then drizzle with oil.

Bake in the oven for about 20 minutes, until the fish is just cooked.

Serve with a lemon wedge on top of each fillet, and a part-baked baguette.

TIP

You can't have too much basil, so top with homegrown fresh basil leaves if you've grown some (see page 13).

HONEY MUSTARD SAUSAGE TRAYBAKE

Everyone knows that honey and mustard go well together, but combining them with sausages for this traybake was an inspired choice (if I do say so myself). I couldn't be happier with how this recipe turned out.

10 mins prep • 30 mins cooking • Serves 4

4 tbsp honey

4 tbsp mustard

1 tbsp oil

8 sausages

4 sweet potatoes, cut into chunks

1 onion, cut into wedges

200g frozen mixed peppers

500g frozen casserole veg

Salt and pepper, to taste

Preheat the oven to 200°C/Fan 180°C/Gas 6.

Mix the honey, mustard and oil in a large bowl, then add the sausages, potatoes and vegetables, and stir to mix.

Tip everything onto a large baking tray, spreading it out evenly. Pour over any remaining dressing.

Season with salt and pepper, and bake in the oven for 30 minutes.

Once out of the oven, slice the sausages lengthways, then into chunks before serving.

TIP
Slicing the cooked sausages is a little cheat to make it seem as though there is more meat!

BBQ SAUSAGE TRAYBAKE

Combining BBQ sauce and sausages is a no-brainer, and there is no easier way to do it than in a traybake.

10 mins prep • 30 mins cooking • Serves 4

500g baby potatoes, halved

8 sausages

2 onions, cut into wedges

2 tbsp oil

350g frozen Mediterranean veg

FOR THE BBQ SAUCE:

6 tbsp tomato ketchup

2 tbsp soft brown sugar

2 tbsp honey

2 tbsp sweet chilli sauce

1 tbsp Worcestershire sauce

2 garlic cloves, crushed

1 tsp mustard (optional)

1 tsp onion powder or onion salt

Preheat the oven to 200°C/Fan 180°C/Gas 6.

Parboil the baby potatoes for 5 minutes.

Meanwhile, add all the BBQ sauce ingredients into a pot and heat through until the sugar has melted. Allow to cool.

Once the sauce has cooled, stir in the sausages and onion wedges, and allow them to marinate a little.

When your potatoes have parboiled, drain them and return to the pot. Add the veg, pour in the oil and stir thoroughly to coat everything.

Transfer the potato/veg mixture to a large oven tray and pour over the BBQ and sausage sauce, mixing well until everything is well coated.

Put in the oven for 30 minutes, stirring halfway through. Once cooked, serve with some fresh basil leaves (if you have grown them).

SWEET CHILLI CHICKEN TRAYBAKE

If you love sweet chilli – and let's face it, what's not to love?
– this will be a sure-fire hit for you and your family.

10 mins prep • 30 mins cooking • Serves 4

500g baby potatoes, halved

2 tbsp oil

4 tbsp sweet chilli sauce

2 chicken breasts, diced

2 onions, cut into wedges

350g frozen Mediterranean veg

Preheat the oven to 200°C/Fan 180°C/Gas 6.

Parboil the baby potatoes for 5 minutes.

Meanwhile, add 1 tablespoon of the oil and all of the sweet chilli sauce to a bowl and mix well.

Stir the chicken and onion wedges into the sauce and allow to marinate while the potatoes are parboiling.

Drain the potatoes and return to the pot. Pour in the remainder of the oil and stir thoroughly to ensure the potatoes are coated.

Put the chicken, onions, potatoes and frozen veg on a large baking tray. Mix well until everything is coated in the sauce, then spread out evenly.

Cook in the oven for 30 minutes, then serve.

TIP

For an extra pop of colour and flavour, top with homegrown fresh basil leaves (see page 13).

CAJUN CHICKEN TRAYBAKE

Sweet potatoes, chicken and Cajun spices are a match made in heaven, so this traybake will definitely hit the spot.

5 mins prep • 30 mins cooking • Serves 4

2 tbsp oil

2 tbsp Cajun seasoning

2 chicken breasts, diced

2 onions, cut into wedges

500g sweet potatoes, cut into wedges

350g frozen stir-fry veg

Preheat the oven to 200°C/Fan 180°C/Gas 6.

Add the oil and Cajun seasoning to a small bowl, mixing well.

Put the chicken, onions, sweet potatoes and frozen veg on a large baking tray.

Pour over the oil and spice mix, stirring until everything is well coated.

Bake in the oven for 30 minutes, then serve.

TIP

With its cayenne and chilli powder, Cajun seasoning can be spicy – so beware!

MAPLE-GLAZED PORK TRAYBAKE

Yes, this is as good as it sounds! The syrup and the pork combine to create a dish that is not just sweet but also has a smoky kick to it.

5 mins prep • 45 mins cooking • Serves 4

250g maple syrup

170g tomato ketchup

120ml cold water

½ tsp onion salt

¼ tsp celery salt

¼ tsp pepper

4 pork loin chops

200g frozen mixed peppers

350g frozen Mediterranean veg

2 onions, quartered

250g cherry tomatoes

500g baby potatoes, halved

Preheat the oven to 200°C/Fan 180°C/Gas 6.

Mix the maple syrup, ketchup, water, onion salt, celery salt and pepper in a bowl.

Put the pork and all the veg, including the onions, tomatoes and potatoes, on a large baking tray. Pour over the sauce.

Bake in the oven for 45 minutes, then serve.

PORK LOIN TRAYBAKE

This meaty Med-style traybake is simply, yet deliciously,
flavoured with garlic, oregano and paprika. Mouth-watering and cheap to make
– what more could you want?

10 mins prep • 30 mins cooking • Serves 4

500g baby potatoes

4 pork loin chops

2 onions, quartered

350g frozen
   Mediterranean veg

350g cherry tomatoes

4 garlic cloves, sliced

1 tbsp dried oregano

1 tbsp paprika

Salt and pepper, to taste

1 tbsp oil

Preheat the oven to 180°C/Fan 160°C/Gas 4.

Parboil the baby potatoes for 5 minutes, then drain.

Place the loin chops on a large baking tray.

Add all the veg, including the parboiled potatoes, to a
bowl and mix them up, then add the garlic, oregano,
paprika, seasoning and oil, and toss together before
putting it all onto the tray with the chops, in an even
layer.

Cook in the oven for 30 minutes, then serve.

TIP
You can use lamb chops
in this dish, if you
would prefer.

BEEF & CHORIZO TRAYBAKE

Knowing what to do with beef, other than a stew, can be a struggle. Teaming it up with chorizo in this traybake turned out to be a successful experiment, I think you'll agree.

15 mins prep • 45 mins cooking • Serves 4

1 tbsp oil

500g stir-fry beef strips or
   thin-cut steaks, sliced

1 tbsp plain flour

500g baby potatoes

2 onions, quartered

100g frozen sliced
   peppers

250g cherry tomatoes

100g chorizo, diced

1 tsp chilli flakes

1–2 tsp smoked paprika

½ tsp dried oregano

2–3 garlic cloves, crushed

Preheat the oven to 180°C/Fan 160°C/Gas 4.

Add a splash of oil to a frying pan, coat the beef in the flour, and then fry until browned.

Meanwhile, parboil the baby potatoes for about 5 minutes, then drain.

Put the beef, potatoes, onions, peppers, tomatoes and chorizo into a large roasting tray.

Mix the oil, chilli flakes, smoked paprika, oregano and garlic together in a small bowl, then pour over the meat and veg and stir until everything is coated thoroughly.

Bake in the oven for 45 minutes, then serve.

MEAT
& FISH

LEMON CHICKEN

This could well have gone into the Fakeaways section, but it sits just as comfortably here. It's a speedy classic that's light, refreshing and tasty.

2 mins prep • 18 mins cooking • Serves 4

3 chicken breasts

Salt and pepper, to taste

1 tbsp oil

3 tbsp fresh tarragon, chopped

350g frozen stir-fry veg

500ml chicken stock

4 egg yolks

3 tbsp lemon juice

Cooked rice, to serve

Season the chicken breasts with salt and pepper.

Heat the oil in a large pan and cook the chicken for about 8 minutes, until browned, turning frequently. Drain off any excess fat.

Add the tarragon, stir-fry veg and stock, and cook for a further 5 minutes or until the chicken is cooked through.

Whisk together the egg yolks and lemon juice, then gradually add to the chicken, stirring constantly.

Cook for another 5 minutes, stirring until you get a smooth, thickened sauce.

Season with salt and pepper, slice the chicken and serve with rice cooked as per the packet instructions.

TIP
Cooking the breasts whole will prevent them from drying out.

BEEF STROGANOFF

Using beef stir-fry strips in this stroganoff means that it doesn't need to be cooked for too long, making it perfect for a midweek treat.

2 mins prep • 16 mins cooking • Serves 4

2 tbsp oil

1 tbsp butter

1 onion, diced

200g mushrooms, thickly sliced

400g beef stir-fry strips

¼ tsp salt

¼ tsp black pepper

240ml double cream

160ml sour cream

¼ tsp paprika

Cooked rice or pasta, to serve

Heat 1 tablespoon of the oil and all of the butter in a large frying pan over a medium-high heat, until the butter starts to foam.

Add the onion and cook for 5 minutes, stirring often, until it starts to soften.

Add the mushrooms and cook for a further 3–4 minutes, stirring often, until lightly browned.

Transfer the contents of the pan to a heatproof bowl. Place the pan back over the heat and turn the heat up to high.

Drizzle the strips of steak with the remaining tablespoon of oil, sprinkle with the salt and pepper, and place in the hot pan, in a single layer. Cook for 1 minute, then turn the strips over and cook for a further 30 seconds.

Add the onion and mushrooms back to the pan, and lower to a medium-low heat.

Pour in the double cream, followed by the sour cream. Stir and slowly heat through until the sauce is hot and the sauce at the edge of the pan is just starting to bubble (don't let it boil). Turn off the heat.

Spoon the stroganoff over cooked rice or pasta, and sprinkle with the paprika just before serving.

TIP

Chopped, fresh parsley provides the ideal finish to this dish – see page 13 for growing your own.

SUMMERY FISH STEW

I love this light and refreshing fish stew. It is so simple to make and tastes amazing.
Serve with chunks of warm part-baked bread.

5 mins prep • 10 mins cooking • Serves 4

1 tbsp oil

3 spring onions, chopped

2 tins of chopped
    tomatoes, or 800ml
    tomato base sauce
    (page 217)

400g frozen
    Mediterranean veg

3 frozen white fish fillets

1 lemon, halved

Fresh basil leaves to
    garnish

Part-baked baguette, to
    serve

Heat the oil in a large, deep frying pan over a high heat.
Add the spring onion, tomatoes and the Mediterranean
veg.

Simmer for 3–5 minutes.

Reduce the heat to medium and add the fish fillets so that
they are partially submerged in the tomato sauce. Cover
with a lid and allow to cook for 4–5 minutes, depending
on the thickness of the fish.

Check to see if your fish is cooked through. If not, give it
another couple of minutes.

Squeeze the lemon juice into the pan, stir gently but
thoroughly, and serve sprinkled with basil leaves.

feelin'
fancy?

*Add a glass of white wine when you add the
tomatoes and veg.*

SAUSAGE CHILLI WITH CREAMY CHIVE CRUSHED POTATOES

Using sausages instead of mince for this dish makes a cheaper and, in my opinion, tastier dish – and the creamy chive mashed potatoes are to die for. I'm confident this will become a favourite in your house, as it is in mine.

5 mins prep • 15 mins cooking • Serves 4

1kg new potatoes, skins on, thickly sliced

8 sausages

2 tsp vegetable oil

200g frozen mixed peppers

200g frozen Mediterranean veg

2 garlic cloves, crushed

1 tsp ground coriander

1 tsp chilli powder

1 tsp ground cumin

1 x 400g tin red kidney beans

2 x 400g tins chopped tomatoes or 800ml tomato base sauce (page 217)

2 tsp sugar

5 tbsp plain yoghurt

20g fresh chives, snipped

Put the potatoes on to boil for 10 minutes, until tender.

Meanwhile, squeeze three balls of meat from each sausage (discarding the skins), then fry in the oil for 5 minutes, until lightly browned all over.

Add the peppers and veg to the pan with the meatballs, then fry for 4 minutes more.

Tip in the garlic and spices, fry for 1 minute, then mix in the beans (drained and rinsed), tomatoes and sugar.

Simmer for 5 minutes, stirring occasionaly, until the saucy and meatballs are cooked.

Meanwhile, drain the potatoes, then mash in the pan. Fold through the yoghurt and chives, loosen with a splash of water, then serve with the sausage chilli.

feelin' fancy?

Top with a dollop more yoghurt and a sprinkling of chives to make a real feast for the eyes.

CRISPY PORK SCHNITZEL

Despite the fancy name, this is just a simple but different way of serving up pork
– without the obligatory apple or cider!

5 mins prep • 8 mins cooking • Serves 4

120g plain flour

2 eggs

1 tbsp milk

70g breadcrumbs

½ tsp salt

½ tsp pepper

4 pork loin chops

3 tbsp oil

Peppercorn sauce, to
serve (page 216)

Mashed potato, to serve

Cooked vegetables, to
serve

To prepare the pork, first set up three bowls. Fill one with
the flour, one with the eggs and milk (whisked together),
and one with the breadcrumbs and the salt and pepper
mixed in.

Dip each pork chop in the flour, then the egg, then the
breadcrumb bowl to coat it fully.

Heat the oil in a large frying pan over a medium-high
heat. Add the coated pork and cook until golden brown,
approximately 3–4 minutes on each side.

Serve with pepper sauce (made using the white sauce on
page 216), mashed potato and mixed veg.

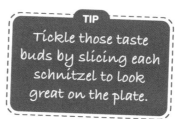

TIP
Tickle those taste
buds by slicing each
schnitzel to look
great on the plate.

WHITE FISH & COLCANNON

This fish dish is lightly flavoured but delicious. I have cheated a bit to call this colcannon when there's no potato, but hey, it's my book!

5 mins prep • 10 mins cooking • Serves 4

3 frozen white fish fillets

50g butter

2 tsp thyme

1 lemon, quartered

Salt and pepper, to taste

½ pack cooking bacon, diced

200g frozen cabbage

2 x 400g tins butter beans

100ml cream

Preheat the oven to 220°C/Fan 200°C/Gas 7.

Cut out four squares of baking paper.

Halve one of the fish fillets (for the kids) and then add one fillet to the centre of each piece of baking paper.

Put 10g of butter on each fillet, along with half a teaspoon of thyme and a lemon quarter.

Season with salt and pepper, then fold the paper over and make a parcel by twisting the top.

Put on a baking tray and bake in the oven for 10 minutes.

Meanwhile, heat a large frying pan over a medium heat, then fry the diced bacon for 2 minutes.

Add the remaining butter and the cabbage to the bacon pan and cook for a further 5 minutes.

Tip the (drained and rinsed) butter beans into the bacon and cabbage, and roughly mash with a potato masher.

Stir thoroughly, then add the cream (and a splash of water, milk or extra cream as needed, for the desired consistency) and heat through.

Remove the fish from the oven and serve over or alongside the butter-bean colcannon.

STEAMED FISH WITH COUSCOUS PARCELS

Once served up, this dish looks like it's taken a lot more time and effort to prepare than it actually did. Dare I say, fine dining at its freshest and simplest? I think so.

10 mins prep • 15 mins cooking • Serves 4

200g couscous

6 spring onions, thinly sliced

1 tbsp lemon juice

1 tsp ground cumin

400ml boiling water

2 tbsp parsley, roughly chopped

2 tbsp coriander leaves, roughly chopped

350g cherry tomatoes, halved

Salt and pepper, to taste

Olive oil, for brushing and drizzling

3 frozen white fish fillets

1 lemon, thinly sliced into wedges, to garnish

Preheat the oven to 200°C/Fan 180°C/Gas 6.

Place the couscous, spring onion, lemon juice and cumin in a large, heatproof bowl. Pour the water over the couscous, cover tightly with heatproof cling film and set aside for 5 minutes.

Stir in the parsley, coriander and cherry tomatoes, and toss to fluff up the couscous. Season well with salt and pepper.

Tear off four sheets of foil or baking paper, each around 45cm in length. Brush the centre of each with a little olive oil and place one quarter of the couscous in the centre of each sheet. Top with a fish fillet – half a fillet each for the kids. Drizzle with a little oil and add a slice of lemon on the fillet. Season the fish well with salt and pepper.

Bring the edges of the foil or paper over to enclose the fish, and seal well by folding the edges over. Make sure you leave some air space in the parcels – they should be sealed securely but not wrapped tightly.

Place the fish parcels on a large baking sheet and bake in the oven for about 15 minutes (the parcels should have puffed up a little). Serve on warm plates with more lemon wedges.

CORNED BEEF HASH

Corned beef was my dad's favourite when I was growing up. I'm sure if he were still with us he would be a big fan of this dish.

....

2 mins prep • 15 mins cooking • Serves 4

4 potatoes, cubed – or leftover cooked potatoes, 2 tins new potatoes or 1 pre-cooked jacket potato

2 tbsp oil

1 onion, diced

1 garlic clove, crushed

Salt and pepper, to taste

1 tin corned beef, cubed

1 tin baked beans

Dash of Worcestershire sauce

A little grated Cheddar cheese (optional)

1 or 2 eggs per person, fried or poached

Parboil your potatoes for 5 minutes, then drain. Skip this step if using leftover, tinned or pre-cooked potatoes.

Heat the oil in a large frying pan and fry the onion until it begins to soften. Add the garlic and seasoning, then stir well.

Add the potatoes and fry for another 5 minutes, before adding the corned beef, baked beans and Worcestershire sauce. Stir well again.

Pour the mixture into an ovenproof dish, sprinkle with cheese (if using) and put under a preheated hot grill until crispy, or the cheese has melted.

Serve each portion topped with an egg or two.

TIP

Garnish with homegrown fresh chives – see page 13.

HAM HASH

This is a great recipe for using up any leftover ham. If you don't have any, then you can boil up a ham hock and use the stock for soup, or the Ham & Egg Rice on page 119, and the meat for this dish.

2 mins prep • 17 mins cooking • Serves 4

4 potatoes, cubed –
or leftover cooked
potatoes, 2 tins new
potatoes or 1 pre-
cooked jacket potato

25g butter

250g frozen cabbage

1 onion, thinly sliced

100ml vegetable stock

200g leftover ham,
shredded

If using raw potatoes, parboil them in a large pan of boiling water, then drain.

Melt half the butter in a large frying pan. Throw in the cabbage and onion and fry for a couple of minutes.

Add the stock and cook for 5 more minutes, until the veg is starting to soften. Stir in the ham and potatoes and push down in the pan to flatten slightly.

Cook for 8 minutes until the base is golden and crisp.

Preheat the grill on high. Dot the remaining butter on top of the hash, then pop under the hot grill for a couple of minutes, until golden and crispy.

feelin' fancy?

Serve with baked beans and a runny-yolk egg.

SALMON HASH

Using leftover or tinned potatoes and tinned salmon means this meal is cheap,
quick and something a wee bit different.

2 mins prep • 18 mins cooking • Serves 4

4 potatoes, cubed –
   or leftover cooked
   potatoes, 2 tins new
   potatoes or 1 pre-
   cooked jacket potato

1 tbsp oil

100g spring onions, thinly
   sliced

1 x 400g tin salmon,
   drained with bones
   removed

Fresh dill, chopped, to
   taste

1 lemon

Parboil your potatoes for 5 minutes, then drain. Skip this
step if using leftovers, tinned or pre-cooked.

Heat the oil in a large frying pan over a medium heat,
then add your potatoes and spring onion and fry for a
couple of minutes.

Add the flaked salmon and stir through, then cook for
5 minutes, until the base is golden and crisp.

Sprinkle over the dill and lemon zest.

Preheat the grill on high and place the pan underneath
until the hash is golden and crispy, then serve.

*Serve this dish with a runny-yolked egg
(fried or poached) or two for an extra treat.*

CHORIZO & SAUSAGE HASH

I love a good hash. It's a great way to use up leftover potatoes and small amounts of meat and veg. This one is a favourite of mine because I love anything with chorizo.

2 mins prep • 14 mins cooking • Serves 4

4 potatoes, cubed – or leftover cooked potatoes, 2 tins new potatoes or 1 pre-cooked jacket potato

2 tbsp oil

2 sausages

150g chorizo, diced

2 onions, diced

1 tbsp paprika

50g Cheddar cheese, grated

Parboil your potatoes for 5 minutes, then drain. Skip this step if using leftovers, tinned or pre-cooked.

Heat the oil in a large frying pan. Squeeze the meat from each sausage (discarding the skins). Fry the chorizo, onion and sausage meat for 5 minutes, until cooked through.

Sprinkle the paprika into the pan and cook for 1 minute.

Add your potatoes and cook for 10 minutes, until crispy.

Sprinkle the cheese on top and put under a preheated hot grill until melted.

Serve with fried or poached eggs or baked beans, or both.

feelin' fancy?

Serve with fried or poached eggs or baked beans, or both.

SLOW COOKER BBQ PULLED CHICKEN

This dish is just as good as you think it's going to be. Good luck saving any leftovers!

10 mins prep • 6–8 hours cooking • Serves 8

3 chicken breasts

250ml tomato ketchup

2 tbsp mustard

2 tsp lemon juice

4 garlic cloves, crushed

125ml syrup

2 tbsp Worcestershire sauce

½ tsp chilli powder

⅛ tsp cayenne pepper

2 dashes of hot sauce

Place the chicken breasts in the bottom of the slow cooker.

In a bowl, mix together all the other ingredients, then pour over the chicken.

Put the slow cooker on a low heat, cover and cook for 6–8 hours.

Remove the chicken breasts, shred with a fork, then return to the sauce and mix.

Serve on a roll with salad or on a jacket potato.

PHILLY CHEESESTEAK BAGUETTES

This one will set your taste buds alight – it's a little punch of flavour
in a deceptively simple package.

2 mins prep • 15 mins cooking • Serves 4

1 tbsp oil

1 onion, thinly sliced

150g frozen mixed
  peppers

3 tsp crushed garlic

Salt and pepper, to taste

9 slices of cooked beef

3 part-baked crusty
  baguettes (1 per adult;
  ½ per child)

3 slices of cheese, halved

Heat the oil in a large frying pan over a medium heat,
then add the onions and fry for 4 minutes.

Add the peppers and continue to cook until they start to
caramelise.

Add the garlic and seasoning, then cook for another
minute.

Push the mix to one side of the pan and add the slices of
beef, turning the meat over until it is warmed through.

Mix the meat with the onions and peppers, and leave over
a low heat.

Bake the baguettes in the oven as per the packet
instructions, then cut down the middle of each and
remove a little of the insides (save for breadcrumbs).

In the pan, separate the meat mixture into four portions
and top with the cheese slices. When the cheese has
melted, carefully remove each portion with a fish slice and
place inside the baguettes. Serve hot.

FAKEAWAYS

SLOW COOKER PEANUT CHICKEN

This is one of my favourite recipes as it is so easy to make and super tasty. I often double or even triple the ingredients to make some homemade ready meals, as I just can't get enough of it.

10 mins prep • 4 hours cooking • Serves 4

3 chicken breasts, diced

2 onions, diced

2 garlic cloves, crushed

200g frozen mixed
    peppers

200g frozen baby carrots

120g peanut butter

1 tbsp cornflour

2 tbsp lime juice

2 tbsp soy sauce

1 tbsp curry powder

1 red chilli, diced

1 tin chopped tomatoes
    or 400ml tomato base
    sauce (page 217)

Cooked rice, to serve

Add all the ingredients to the slow cooker and stir thoroughly.

Cover and cook on low for 4 hours.

Serve with rice, cooked as per packet instructions.

TIP
Garnish with homegrown coriander (see page 13).

FISH CURRY

Growing up, I don't remember eating a lot of fish, so I had to work hard to make sure I introduced plenty into our diet. Someone told me that white fish can be treated as just another meat, and this made it easier for me to diversify our menu. I would urge you to give this one a go even if you're not initially convinced. The fusion of fish and curry might surprise you.

2 mins prep • 18 mins cooking • Serves 4

1 tbsp oil

1 onion, sliced

200g frozen mixed peppers

2–3 red chillies, finely chopped

2 garlic cloves, sliced

1 tsp mustard seeds

1 tsp ground coriander

½ tsp ground turmeric

½ tsp chilli powder

Thumb-sized piece of ginger, grated

1 x 400ml tin coconut milk

175ml water

500g frozen white fish fillets, defrosted

Salt and pepper, to taste

Cooked rice, to serve

Heat the oil in a large frying pan, add the onion and fry for 2 minutes.

Add in the peppers, chillies (add more or less depending how hot you like it), garlic and mustard seeds, and fry for another 3 minutes.

Add the ground coriander, turmeric, chilli powder and ginger, and fry for another minute.

Now add the coconut milk and water, bring gently to the boil and then and simmer for about 10 minutes, until the sauce has thickened slightly.

Cut the fish into chunks. Season the curry with the salt and pepper, add in the fish, cover, and simmer gently for 4–5 minutes or until the fish is just cooked.

Serve with rice, cooked as per the packet instructions.

CHIPOTLE CHICKEN

This Mexican-inspired chicken dish is very flavoursome. It's a sort of sweet
but smoky BBQ flavour, which is a firm favourite with my son, Kyle. And, for me,
a happy Kyle is a happy house.

5 mins prep • 30 mins cooking • Serves 4

1 tbsp vegetable oil

1 onion, diced

3 garlic cloves, crushed

200g frozen mixed
peppers

½ tsp soft brown sugar

1 tsp chipotle paste

1 x 400g tin chopped
tomatoes or 400ml
tomato base sauce
(page 217)

2 large chicken breasts

Cooked rice, to serve

Heat the oil in a large frying pan and fry the onion for
5 minutes.

Add the garlic and peppers, and cook for 3 minutes more.

Stir in the sugar, chipotle paste and tomatoes, then add
the chicken breasts.

Simmer for 20 minutes, until the chicken is cooked.

Remove the chicken and shred with two forks. Add it back
into the sauce and stir well.

Serve with rice, cooked as per the packet instructions.

TIP

Chopped fresh
coriander is the perfect
garnish to this dish –
see page 13 for tips on
growing your own.

LENTIL DAHL

Looking at the ingredients list here, you might think this meal is just a page filler – lentils? Water? But I promise you, once you've tasted it, you'll know exactly why it's here.

5 mins prep • 40 mins cooking • Serves 4

1 tbsp oil

1 onion, diced

3 garlic cloves, crushed

2 tsp ground ginger

½ tsp chilli flakes

½ tsp ground cinnamon

1 tsp ground coriander

300g split red lentils

1l water

Flatbreads, to serve

Heat the oil in a large frying pan over a medium heat, then fry the onion until soft, about 5 minutes.

Add the garlic and spices, and fry for another 2 minutes.

Add the lentils and stir until coated in the spices.

Cover with the water, bring to the boil then reduce the heat and simmer for 30 minutes, stirring occasionaly, until thick and all the liquid has been absorbed.

Serve with homemade flatbreads, which you can find the recipe for in my previous book.

> **TIP**
> A little fresh coriander on top will go a long way in terms of flavour – why not grow your own (see page 13)?

MANDARIN & CHICKPEA CURRY

Wow, weird combo, right? Surprisingly, it works! I'm not 100 per cent sure why, but it does. And it's another vegan recipe to have up your sleeve.

2 mins prep • 18 mins cooking • Serves 4

1 tbsp oil

1 onion, chopped

3 garlic cloves, crushed

½ tsp cumin seeds

½ tsp mustard seeds

1 tsp ground turmeric

1 tsp ground cumin

1 tsp ground coriander

1 tsp chilli powder

1 tsp salt

1 tbsp tomato puree

2 tins chickpeas

1 tin chopped tomatoes

200g frozen cauliflower

200g frozen broccoli

250ml vegetable stock

1 tin mandarins in juice

1 tsp garam masala

Cooked rice, to serve

Heat the oil in a large frying pan over a medium heat. Add the onion, garlic, cumin seeds and mustard seeds and cook for 3–5 minutes, or until the onion has softened.

Add the ground turmeric, cumin, coriander, chilli powder and salt.

Stir in the tomato puree and cook for 2 minutes.

Stir in the (drained and rinsed) chickpeas, tomatoes, veg and vegetable stock.

Bring to the boil, then reduce the heat and simmer for 10 minutes.

Add the drained mandarins and heat through.

Remove from the heat and mix in the garam masala.

Serve with rice, cooked as per the packet instructions.

BEEF & POTATO CURRY

I first made this curry because I had beef left over from our Sunday roast. It was such a hit that it became a regular fixture on my meal plan.

2 mins prep • 18 mins cooking • Serves 4

2 tbsp oil

2 onions, diced

400g beef sizzle steaks, diced

4 garlic cloves, crushed

2cm piece of ginger, grated

1 tsp chilli flakes

2 tbsp ground coriander

2 tbsp curry powder

2 tbsp tomato puree

1 sweet potato, chopped into chunks

1 large potato, chopped into chunks

200g frozen mixed peppers

1 x 400ml tin coconut milk

1 x 400g tin chopped tomatoes or 400ml tomato base sauce (page 217)

1 tbsp lime juice

Cooked rice, to serve

Heat the oil in a large pan and fry the onions and diced beef over a medium heat for 3 minutes.

Add the garlic, ginger, chilli flakes, coriander and curry powder, then mix well and cook for another minute.

Add the tomato puree and stir to combine. Then add the potatoes, peppers, coconut milk and tomatoes, cover the pan and gently bring to the boil. Reduce the heat and allow to simmer for 15 minutes.

Add the lime juice, give it another stir and serve with rice, cooked per the packet instructions.

> **TIP**
> Fresh coriander, chopped, makes the perfect garnish — grow your own to save those pennies (see page 13).

SWEET & SOUR VEG STIR-FRY

This recipe is one of the quickest, easiest meat-free meals that I make on a regular basis. Plenty of veg and a spicy, tangy sweet and sour sauce combine to make this meal seem much more than the sum of its parts.

2 mins prep • 10 mins cooking • Serves 4

2 tbsp tomato ketchup

2 tbsp vinegar

2 tsp sugar

50ml water

1 tsp cornflour

1 tbsp oil

750g frozen stir-fry vegetables

100g frozen pineapple chunks

Cooked rice, to serve

Whisk the sauce ingredients – the ketchup, vinegar, sugar, water and cornflour – together in a bowl.

Heat the oil in a wok, then stir-fry the veg for 5 minutes over a high heat.

Pour the sauce over the veg and stir-fry for another 2–3 minutes.

Add the pineapple chunks and stir-fry for a further 2 minutes.

Serve with rice, cooked per the packet instructions.

feelin' fancy?

Stir in some diced cooked meat.

SAUCY SATAY CHICKEN NOODLES

Who doesn't love a saucy satay? This cheeky chicken dish, served with noodles, is a definite treat for everyone – and it's so cheap and easy to make.

4 mins prep • 14 mins cooking • Serves 4

2 tbsp soy sauce

2 tsp cornflour

3 chicken breasts, diced

1 tbsp oil

200g frozen mixed peppers

350g frozen stir-fry vegetables

4 spring onions, chopped

2 tbsp ground ginger

4 tbsp peanut butter

1 tbsp sweet chilli sauce

1 tin coconut milk

4 noodle nests

2 tbsp lime juice

Pinch of salt and pepper

Pop the soy sauce and cornflour in a mixing bowl. Stir to dissolve.

Add the diced chicken and mix well to coat in the marinade.

Heat the oil in a large saucepan or wok over a high heat.

Add the peppers, stir-fry veg, spring onions and ginger. Stir-fry for 1 minute.

Add the chicken and cook for another 3–4 minutes, until lightly browned all over.

Stir in the peanut butter, sweet chilli sauce and coconut milk.

Bring to the boil, then reduce to a simmer for about 4–5 minutes, until the chicken is cooked through and the sauce has thickened slightly.

Meanwhile, cook the noodles according to the packet instructions and add to the stir-fry. Stir together until piping hot.

Add the lime juice and salt and pepper, then serve.

TIP
Serve in bowls with a sprinkle of fresh coriander on top if you've grown your own (see page 13) and/or some extra spring onion, finely chopped.

HONEY, GARLIC & SOY CHICKEN STIR-FRY

I love a stir-fry. They are so easy and quick, and you can mix up the flavours/ingredients to your own personal taste, or to suit what's in your cupboards and fridge.

5 mins prep • 10 mins cooking • Serves 4

1 tbsp oil

500g boneless chicken thighs, cut into chunks or slices

3 garlic cloves, crushed

3 tbsp soy sauce

2 tbsp honey

350g frozen stir-fry vegetables

4 noodle nests

Heat the oil in a wok or large frying pan and fry the chicken for 3–4 minutes over a high heat, stirring all the time.

Add the garlic and toss, then add the soy sauce and honey.

Stir to coat all the meat. Cook for another couple of minutes, until the chicken is cooked through and the sauce has reduced slightly.

Add in the veg and stir-fry for 2–3 minutes. You want the veg crispy, not soggy.

Meanwhile, cook the noodles according to the packet instructions.

Serve the stir-fry on a bed of noodles.

TIP

Garnish with chopped spring onion, if you fancy, for added authenticity.

VEGAN BEAN BURGERS

As veganism grows, you never know when you're going to be entertaining guests
who follow a plant-based diet, so it's great to have this recipe up your sleeve.
Tasty, nutritional and quick equals a winner, in my book.

....

10 mins prep • 6 mins cooking • Makes 4

½ onion, diced

1 tin mixed beans

2 slices of vegan bread
   (crumbled)

½ tsp salt

1 tsp garlic powder

1 tsp onion powder

60g plain flour

Salt and pepper, to taste

2 tbsp oil

Vegan bread rolls, to
   serve

Fry the onion in a frying pan over a medium heat until
soft, about 3–5 minutes.

In a large bowl, mash the (drained and rinsed) beans until
almost smooth. Add the onions, along with the crumbled
bread, salt, garlic powder and onion powder, mixing to
combine well.

Add the flour a few tablespoons at a time and mix well
to combine. Your veggie burger mixture will be very thick
(you may want to use your hands to work the flour
in well). Season with salt and pepper.

Divide and form the bean mixture into four individual
patties, just over 1cm thick each. The best way to do this
is to roll a handful into a ball, then flatten it gently.

Fry your bean patties in the oil over a medium-low heat
until slightly firm and lightly browned on each side, about
3 minutes each side. If your pan is too hot, your bean
burgers will brown too quickly and not be heated through
or cooked in the middle, so adjust the heat and cooking
time as needed.

Serve in a toasted vegan bread roll.

TIP

Bump up the healthy
eating points – and
flavours – by adding
some lettuce leaves and
tomato slices.

SLOW COOKER VEGGIE SLOPPY JOES

This is an ideal store cupboard meal, which makes it super-cheap, and because it's done in the slow cooker, it's super-easy too. The perfect Friday night fakeaway, without any real effort.

10 mins prep • 5½ (on high)–8½ (on low) hours cooking • Serves 4

2 tins chickpeas, drained and rinsed

100g dried split red lentils, rinsed

1 onion, diced

3 garlic cloves, diced

1 tin chopped tomatoes

120ml water

60ml apple cider vinegar

50g soft brown sugar

3 tbsp Worcestershire sauce

½ tsp mustard powder

¼ tsp chilli flakes

1 tsp salt

¼ tsp black pepper

Jacket potato or buns, to serve

Add all the ingredients to the slow cooker, mix well and then cover.

Cook on low for 8 hours or on high for 5–6 hours, until the lentils are cooked through and the mixture thickens.

Open the slow cooker and, using a potato masher, mash about a third of the filling.

Give it a good stir, replace the lid and let it cook for another 30 minutes or so, until thickened.

Serve on toasted buns or jacket potatoes.

TIP
A garnish of homegrown chives will set this off nicely – see page 13.

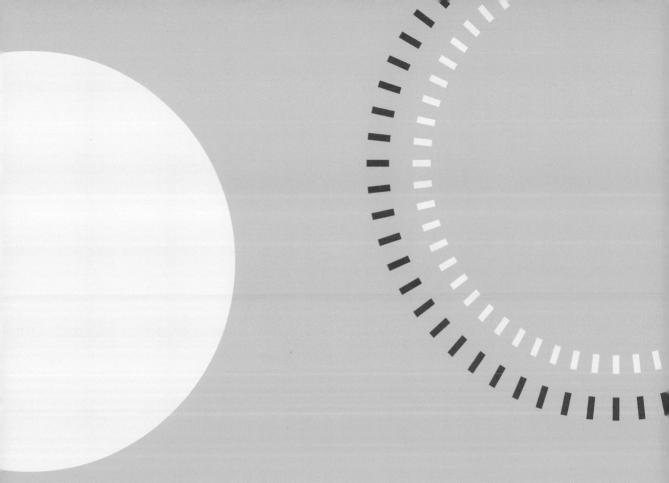

DESSERTS

SLOW COOKER RICE PUDDING

I've always loved rice pudding, and I can't believe it is so easy to make,
especially when you make it in the slow cooker. Served with a big dollop of jam,
this is the ultimate in comfort eating.

5 mins prep • 2^1/$_2$–3 hours cooking • Serves 4

225g pudding rice

1.5l milk

4 tbsp sugar

1 tsp vanilla essence

Add everything to the slow cooker and stir well.

Cover and cook on high for 2^1/$_2$–3 hours, then serve.
Can be enjoyed either hot or cold.

feelin' fancy? Add some dried fruit as well/instead of the jam!

MINI MICROWAVE SPONGE PUDDINGS

Some nights you just want a little something sweet after dinner, and these puddings are the perfect solution. You can be in and out of the kitchen during the ad breaks to make them, then back in front of your favourite programme to eat them.

5 mins prep • 4 mins cooking • Serves 4

125g sugar

125g butter, softened

125g self-raising flour

2 eggs

2 tbsp milk

4 tbsp jam/syrup/honey

Use an electric whisk to combine the sugar, butter, flour, eggs and milk in a mixing bowl, until smooth.

Grease four ramekins or cups and put 1 tablespoon of jam/syrup/honey in the base of each one.

Divide the whisked mixture evenly between the four ramekins/cups, then level the tops.

Cover with cling film and microwave on high for about 4 minutes (check after 3).

Turn the puddings out onto serving plates and enjoy.

feelin' fancy?

Serve with custard for a touch of decadence.

WHITE CHOCOLATE & STRAWBERRY CHEESECAKE

This is my go-to dessert for almost all occasions, and there is never as much as a slice left over. The proof really is in the pudding!

10 mins prep • 2 hours chilling • Serves 8

200g chocolate digestives

100g butter, melted

200g white chocolate

2 x 200g packs soft cheese

250g fresh strawberries, hulled

Crush the chocolate digestives and add them to the melted butter in a pan or bowl.

Mix well, then press the mixture into a greased or lined 20cm square, loose-bottomed baking/cake tin. Refrigerate for 1 hour.

Meanwhile, melt the white chocolate in a heatproof bowl over a pot of gently boiling water. Add the soft cheese and stir well, until smooth and combined.

Cut the strawberries roughly into quarters, add to the chocolate/cheese mixture and mix again.

Pour onto the refrigerated base and spread evenly, then place back in the fridge for another hour before serving.

Eat, and enjoy!

PEANUT BUTTER COOKIES

I can't say anything other than try these, you're gonna love them.

....

8 mins prep • 8 mins cooking • Makes 12

125g peanut butter

110g butter, softened

100g brown sugar

100g white sugar

1 tsp vanilla essence

150g plain flour

½ tsp salt

½ tsp baking powder

½ tsp bicarbonate of soda

Preheat the oven to 180°C/Fan 160°C/Gas 1.

Line a baking tray with baking paper.

In a bowl, mix together the peanut butter, butter, both sugars and vanilla until well combined.

Add all the other ingredients and mix again until totally combined.

Divide and shape the dough into 12 balls, each about 2.5cm in size, and space them out on the baking tray.

Bake in the oven for 8–10 minutes. Leave to sit for 1 minute, then transfer to a wire rack to cool.

CHOC & ORANGE CAKE BARS

My own twist on this infamous treat finally puts to bed the age-old argument of whether this is a cake or a biscuit. It's definitely a cake – no matter what the VAT man says! These do need to be given time to set between steps so bare this in mind when calculating how long you need to make them.

Prep 45 mins • Cook 10 mins • Setting time 4 hours (3 hours plus 2 x 30 mins)

3 eggs

85g sugar

85g self-raising flour

Orange-flavoured jelly

300ml orange juice

4 tbsp orange marmalade

300g dark chocolate, broken into squares

Preheat the oven to 180°C/Fan 160°C/Gas 4. Grease and line the base of an 18cm loose-bottomed, square tin.

Whisk the eggs and sugar together in a bowl until the mixture has at least doubled in size and is thick. Fold in the flour, being careful not to knock out all the air. Pour the mixture into the prepared tin and bake for about 10 minutes (a skewer should come out clean). Leave to cool in the tin for 5 minutes, then turn out onto a wire rack to finish cooling.

Make up the jelly using some of the orange juice (no water), making 300ml. Pour the jelly into an 18cm square tin to set, then refrigerate until set.

Add the marmalade to a small bowl and mix in a splash of orange juice. Spread this on top of your cooled sponge. Put the sponge back in its baking tin and top the marmalade with your set jelly (in one piece).

Melt the chocolate in a bowl over a pan of simmering water. When it has melted, allow to cool slightly before pouring over the jelly, then refrigerate until set again. For a double chocolate layer: once set, add more melted chocolate, then leave to set again in the fridge. You can drizzle this layer for decoration, if desired.

Score into bars and allow to set a final time.

> **TIP**
> Score the bars as soon as possible: if the chocolate sets too hard, it's impossible to cut the bars without them breaking up.

SCOTTISH MACAROON BARS

Okay, I'm going to give you a minute to get over the fact that these bars are made from mashed potato. So now that we're past that, these are very sweet, very moreish, and if you let the kids help, very messy to make. You will need to factor in time for freezing the mix and allowing the chocolate to set when you're making these.

Prep 30 mins • Cook 15 mins • Setting time 5 hours (4 hours plus 1 hour) • Makes 12

114g potato; boiled, peeled and mashed

Approx. 500g icing sugar

150g desiccated coconut, for coating

350g milk chocolate, broken into squares

Preheat the oven to 150°C/Fan 130°C/Gas 2.

Place the cooled mashed potato in a bowl and begin adding the icing sugar, a little at a time. Continue adding the sugar and mixing well, and soon you will have a fondant texture. Add enough sugar so that the mixture comes together and is very stiff, practically impossible to mix.

Line a baking tray with greaseproof paper or a silicone baking mat. Shape the mixture into a rectangle on the tray and freeze for at least 4 hours.

Place half of the shredded coconut on a baking sheet and bake in the oven for 5 minutes until golden brown, stirring regularly. Monitor it closely, as it will brown quickly.

Remove from the oven, cool, then mix with the remaining untoasted coconut. Transfer to a plate for dipping.

Remove the macaroon mixture from the freezer and cut into small bars or balls – they are very sweet.

Melt the chocolate over a pot of hot water. Dip each macaroon piece into the chocolate, then coat immediately with the combination of shredded coconut, then leave to set.

TIP

To get the right texture, use a floury potato such as a Desiree, Estima, King Edward or Maris Piper.

LEMONADE SCONES

Traditional scone recipes can be pretty time-consuming and sometimes very complex.
These lemonade scones are a quick alternative for those last-minute visitors.

5 mins prep • 12 mins cooking • Makes 12

400g self-raising flour,
  plus extra for dusting

175ml double cream

175ml lemonade

Preheat the oven to 220°C/Fan 200°C/Gas 7.

Line a baking tray with baking paper.

Sift the flour into a large bowl. Add the cream and lemonade, stirring until just mixed – don't over-mix, or the scones will be dense.

Tip the mixture onto a lightly floured surface.

Knead three times only, then pat the dough out to a thickness of 2cm.

Cut out circle shapes with a scone cutter and place them on the baking tray.

Keep gently combining the dough offcuts, patting out and cutting again, until there is no dough left.

Bake in the oven for 12–15 minutes, until risen and golden on top. Transfer to a wire rack and leave to cool.

BASICS

MILKS

Shop-bought milk alternatives can be pricey. Who knew that making your own could be so easy? These alternative milks are great for people with allergies or those following certain diets. I find them especially good in smoothies, and I use the coconut milk in curries.

OAT MILK

....

Makes 1 litre

90g porridge oats
1l water

OPTIONAL EXTRAS:
1 tbsp maple syrup
1 tsp vanilla essence
Tiny pinch of salt

Place the oats in a bowl and add enough cold water (not your 1 litre) to cover by about 5cm. Set aside for 15 minutes.

Drain the soaked oats in a fine-mesh sieve (or you can use a clean white T-shirt or a coffee filter) and rinse them thoroughly under running water.

Next, transfer the oats to your blender.

Add half of the measured water, plus the maple syrup, vanilla essence and tiny pinch of salt, if desired. Blend on high speed until the oat milk is smooth, about 1–2 minutes. Add the remaining water and blend again.

To strain, place the fine-mesh sieve over a bowl or wide-necked bottle and pour the mixture through.

Taste, and add more maple syrup for sweetness, if desired.

> **TIP**
>
> Oat milk tastes best after it's been chilled in the fridge for at least 30 minutes, and will keep well in the fridge, covered, for up to 5 days. It will separate over time, so give it a stir before serving.

COCONUT MILK

Makes 500ml

150g desiccated
coconut

375ml very warm water

Line a large, fine-mesh sieve with a double layer of clean white T-shirt and place it over a bowl.

Place the coconut and warm water in a blender and blend on high for 5 minutes. You may want to hold the lid of the blender with a paper towel to prevent spills and burns.

Pour everything through the T-shirt. Gather up the edges and squeeze out as much liquid as you can. Use tongs to squeeze, to prevent burning your hands.

Pour the coconut milk into a jar, cover and store in the fridge for up to 5 days.

RICE MILK

Makes 1 litre

150g cooked, cold
white rice

1l water

Line a large, fine-mesh sieve with a double layer of clean white T-shirt and place it over a bowl.

Add the rice and water to the blender and blitz on high for 1–2 minutes.

Pour everything through the T-shirt. Gather up the edges and squeeze out as much liquid as you can.

Pour the rice milk into a jar, cover and store in the fridge for up to 5 days.

DIPS

HUMMUS

How many times do you find yourself buying tubs of hummus at £1 or more? Or, worse still, find yourself fancying some but there's none in the house? This simple recipe means you'll never have to miss out again – and you can flavour it however you want.

....

Makes 500ml

3 tbsp tahini or peanut
   butter

Juice of 1 lemon

2 garlic cloves, peeled

1 tin chickpeas

1 tsp salt

½ tsp ground cumin

3 tbsp olive oil

2 tbsp water
   (depending on
   consistency)

½ tsp paprika

Put the tahini (or peanut butter) in a processor with the lemon juice and pulse for 1 minute. Add the garlic and blend for another minute.

Add the (drained and rinsed) chickpeas, salt and cumin to the processor and blend until combined.

Drizzle in the olive oil slowly, while the processor is on, and mix until the hummus is of the desired consistency. If it's too thick, add in some water and blend until silky-smooth.

Put in a bowl and top with paprika.

 Add sweet chilli sauce for sweet chilli hummus, or dried red peppers for red pepper hummus.

BASIL PESTO

I used to think that I didn't like pesto, but it turns out I just didn't like it from a jar.
Making your own will really bring out the flavour.

....
Makes 250ml

25g pine nuts

25g Parmesan cheese
(any Italian hard
cheese will do)

2 garlic cloves, peeled

Pinch of salt

50g fresh basil leaves

Juice of 1 lemon

125ml olive oil

Salt and pepper, to
taste

Put a frying pan over a medium heat, add the pine nuts
and toast gently for a couple of minutes.

Finely grate the Parmesan.

Put the garlic and pinch of salt in a food processor and
pulse.

Add the toasted pine nuts and pulse again until roughly
chopped.

Add the basil and pulse carefully until it is mixed well but
still has texture.

Tip into a bowl, add the Parmesan and lemon juice, then
mix.

Gradually stir in the olive oil, mixing it to a juicy paste,
before seasoning to taste.

SAUCES

These sauces are delicious, easy to make and versatile, and are used in many of the recipes in this book. If you look at most brand-name sauces, you'll see they almost all have something extra: garlic, bacon or sweet pepper in a tomato sauce or cheese, parsley or peppercorns in a béchamel. You can jazz up these base sauces, too, by adding extras when reheating, and you'll have a whole range of fancy sauces at your fingertips!

BASIC WHITE SAUCE

This basic white sauce, or béchamel sauce, is the base for all creamy sauces, such as cheese, parsley, peppercorn and mushroom. If you're making a pie filling, you can replace half the milk with stock to give the sauce a bit of flavour that complements the filling perfectly.

....

Makes 500ml

30g butter
30g plain flour
500ml milk

Melt your butter in a pan over a medium heat.

Stir in the flour. It will clump together but don't worry – it's supposed to!

Cook for 2 minutes and then gradually stir in your milk.

Whisk continually until the sauce starts to thicken.

Depending on the end use of your sauce, add any additional ingredients, such as cheese, parsley, peppercorns, etc.

Reduce the heat and simmer for 2 minutes.

TOMATO BASE SAUCE

This sauce transformed my cooking and is loved by my kids, even when they were going through their fussy stages. It is packed full of veg, and one of the great things about it is you can use practically ANY veg. The strong tomato flavour masks the taste of the veg, so no matter how picky your little ones are, they will never know! You can use this sauce whenever a recipe calls for tomato sauce, in place of tinned tomatoes and even on a pizza. I have even started using it in place of tinned tomatoes in most of my recipes. It also makes a delicious dipping sauce.

....

Makes 3 litres

1 tbsp vegetable oil

2 onions, finely diced

100g frozen spinach

50g frozen sliced carrots

200g frozen casserole veg

50g frozen cabbage

2 tins chopped tomatoes

2 tbsp tomato puree

2 tbsp Worcestershire sauce

1 tbsp dried mixed herbs

1¹/₂l beef stock

Sugar, to taste (optional)

Heat the oil in a large pot over a medium heat, add the onions and fry for a few minutes until softened, then chuck everything else into the pot and bring to the boil.

Reduce the heat and leave to simmer for 45 minutes, stirring occasionally, until it is thick and glossy-looking.

Blitz the sauce in the food processor in batches until it is fairly smooth, or use a hand blender.

If your family is used to shop-bought jars, then you should probably have a taste now and stir in some sugar to neutralise the tomatoes, if desired. (Remember: a 500g jar of brand-name sauce often has up to 6 teaspoons of sugar in it, so even if you add a couple of teaspoons, your sauce is still MUCH healthier!)

> **TIP**
> To replicate brand-name sauces, just add the necessary extra ingredient(s) – basil, garlic, chilli, herbs, bacon, sweet pepper – when reheating the sauce. And if you want a creamy tomato sauce, add some of my basic white sauce to it!

BBQ SAUCE

Who doesn't love BBQ sauce? This one can be used in almost every situation. It's perfect to cook meat in, to serve with cooked meat, to be used as a dip or, in Kyle's case, to drench everything he eats!

....

Makes 450ml

250ml tomato ketchup

2 tbsp mustard

2 tsp lemon juice

1 bulb garlic, cloves all crushed

125ml syrup

2 tbsp Worcestershire sauce

½ tsp cayenne pepper

2 dashes of hot sauce

Add all the ingredients to a medium pan over a low heat.

Mix thoroughly and gently bring to the boil.

Simmer for a few minutes, stirring occasionally, until thick and sticky.

CHEAT'S SATAY SAUCE

A quick and easy sauce that can be poured over cooked meat or served as a dip.

....

Makes 100ml

2 tbsp peanut butter

2 tbsp soy sauce

2 tbsp sweet chilli sauce

Add all the ingredients to a small pan over a low heat.

Mix thoroughly and gently bring to the boil, stirring continuously. Add a splash of water, if needed, to thin it a little.

Serve over cooked meat or veg for a quick and easy fakeaway.

CHEAT'S SWEET & SOUR SAUCE

Re-create your favourite takeaway sauce in the comfort of your own home.

....

Makes 100ml

2 tbsp orange
   marmalade

2 tbsp soy sauce

2 tbsp tomato ketchup

1 tsp sugar

½ tbsp white vinegar

Add all the ingredients to a small pan over a low heat.

Mix thoroughly and gently bring to the boil, stirring continuously.

Taste, and add more sweet (sugar) or sour (vinegar) as desired. Add a splash of water, if needed, to thin it.

Serve over cooked meat or veg for a quick and easy fakeaway.

APPLE SAUCE

This recipe is a great addition to smoothies and overnight oats. It can also be added to porridge, rice pudding and lots of other savoury/sweet dishes.

....

Makes 150ml

50g butter

100g frozen apple

1 tsp sugar

Melt the butter in a small pan over a medium heat.

Add the apple and then the sugar.

Cook until softened, stirring occasionally, then mash to a pulp.

INDEX

ACKNOWLEDGEMENTS

The first people I must thank is all the people who bought book one; without you I wouldn't have had the opportunity to write a second book. I really appreciate you spending your hard-earned cash supporting me, and I hope you enjoyed it!

And secondly, I must, again, thank the FYF Facebook community for all their support. I feel like you are all my friends and I love sharing ideas, tips and recipes with you all. I must send a HUGE thank you to Eve for your amazing contributions this year – your recipes are amazing, your pictures are fabulous and your heart of gold shines through in the way you respond to people. You encapsulate everything that it is to be a wee Scottish mammy.

Thank you, Gary and Sam, for your ongoing support. Where would FYF be without you guys? You have both been epic. Warrick, you are THE MAN! Even when you ignore me for days on end, it's always worth the wait. To G, you are going to go far young lady; you are amazingly organised, talented and just the right amount a perfectionist. Thank you for all your help. Kate, although it seems so long ago now, I need to thank you for all your excellent work and your support post-book one release – you're a wee star. And to everyone else in the office, I miss you guys so much. I can't wait to get back to normal and come in for a catch up and a giggle.

Carly Cook, thank you for everything. You make this whole process hassle-free; I couldn't do it without you! My fantastic editor Anna Valentine, who believed in FYF and me from the beginning and has once again been a pleasure to work with. Thank you and congratulations.

The team at Orion have been fabulous again. Thanks to Lucie Stericker, Helen Ewing and Julyan Bayes for their design vision; to Georgia Goodall, for pulling it all together; to Nicole Abel and Helena Fouracre in production and marketing; and to the wonderful Francesca Pearce who I had so much fun working with.

I also have to give a MASSIVE shout out to the incredible photographer, Andrew Hayes-Watkins. Due to Covid-19 and all the lockdown restrictions, we didn't know how or when we would be able to get this book into the studio – until Andrew stepped up and said he would do the cooking, the styling and the photography! How amazing is this guy? Well, you only have to look at the stunning pictures to see; I am genuinely so impressed. Thanks, mate! I'm just gutted I couldn't be there to help out.

Closer to home I have to mention all of my and John's amazing family and friends. Thank you for all your love and support; it's been a tough year, but you have all been fabulous as always.

Ayla, Jamie and Kyle, you will never know how much the mandatory family fun time group video calls got me through lockdown. I love you so much. John, thanks for always doing the dishes without complaining, no matter how many pots and pans I use – at least you get to test all the food! You're my anchor and I love you.

First published in Great Britain in 2021 by Seven Dials
an imprint of The Orion Publishing Group Ltd
Carmelite House, 50 Victoria Embankment
London EC4Y 0DZ

An Hachette UK Company

10 9 8 7 6 5 4 3 2

A CIP catalogue record for this book is
available from the British Library.

ISBN (Trade Paperback) 978 1 8418 8453 0
ISBN (eBook) 978 1 8418 8455 4

Publisher: Anna Valentine
Editor: Georgia Goodall
Photography and Styling: Andrew Hayes-Watkins
Art Direction: Lucie Stericker
Design: Julyan Bayes

Printed in Germany

MIX
Paper from
responsible sources
FSC
www.fsc.org   FSC® C104740

www.orionbooks.co.uk